PLAY THE MAN

PLAY
THE
MAN

BRAD PARK
with Stan Fischler

DODD, MEAD & COMPANY
NEW YORK

Second Printing

ISBN: 0–396–06433–7
Library of Congress Catalog Card Number: 73–181824
Printed in the United States of America
by The Cornwall Press, Inc., Cornwall, N. Y.

796.9
P

To my parents
who helped me reach the NHL
and to Gerry
who hopes I'll stay

Editor's Foreword

After covering the NHL for seventeen years as a professional hockey writer, I can unequivocally report that accounts of games and dressing-room scenes which appear in the daily papers represent only the tip of the reportorial iceberg. Hockey clubs are prone to dispense the self-serving propaganda which will enhance their reputation and speed the turnstile flow. While the players themselves would far rather dash home or elsewhere—than converse with newsmen, most of whom they hold in contempt. Consequently, much of the vital, behind-the-scenes interplay between players, and between players and management, is inevitably ignored unless it is totally inoffensive.

That, in a nutshell, is why I enthusiastically undertook the assignment to collaborate with New York Ranger defenseman Brad Park in his attempt to keep a personal and insightful journal of the recent season. Park had impressed me as being one of the very few NHL players with something to say, and who was willing to say it. Also too, he was an All-Star player on a strong team. So excitement was guaranteed.

Still, writing this book wasn't as easy as flipping the switch on a tape recorder. Brad was compelled to take notes and dictate to his machine at rather difficult moments: after Francis had suspended him; the night he was knocked unconscious by Toronto's Billy MacMillan; and those agonizing hours after Chicago had dispatched the Rangers from the Stanley Cup playoffs. Yet Brad was an ideal subject with whom to work. He never failed to keep an appointment, or to cooperate in a pleasant and enthusiastic manner.

During the course of our collaboration I came to know Brad's parents, Bob and Betty Park, and Brad's wife, Gerry. All wonderful people. I learned, among other things, that Brad was encouraged to pursue hockey by his parents. And, inevitably, I was reminded of the warm support I had always received from my mother and father, both of whom were alive when this book was written.

Unfortunately, my father never lived to see its completion. He died in Brooklyn, New York, at the age of 79 after a long and full life.

One of his great pleasures was watching hockey games—he took me to my first when I was five—and relishing the skills of such classy players as Jean Beliveau, Dave Keon, Henri Richard—and Brad Park. Benjamin Fischler liked a skater who played the game hard but clean. That's why he so enjoyed Brad Park; and that's why I wish to remember him at this time.

STAN FISCHLER

New York City, August 1971

Contents

PLAY THE MAN

I

My Contract

After landing a spot on the National Hockey League's All-Star team my first full season of play, I figured I was entitled to a healthy salary increase over what Emile Francis, the New York Rangers' general manager and coach, was now offering me.

Times have changed in the NHL. Ten years ago it was customary for a player to negotiate with management on his own, face-to-face across the table. But that was before the league expanded, when there was a surplus of players and only six teams. This meant that bosses could tell you to go take a walk if you didn't like what they were offering. Usually the player would then sign for less than he was worth.

Expansion of the NHL from 6 to 12 teams and then to 14 changed the balance of negotiating power, and by 1970 it had become a players' market. Bobby Orr, the Hull brothers and Derek Sanderson were turning to sports attorneys for assistance in negotiating their contracts. This was an important step, because such men as Alan Eagleson of Toronto and Boston's Robert Woolf had a keen idea of a player's value and were also familiar with contractual nuances that might escape a young athlete. I considered engaging each of these attorneys, but since they were both out-of-towners and I was playing and living in New York—during the summer I teach at the Skateland Hockey School in New Hyde Park, Long Island, with my teammate Rod Gilbert—it seemed more practical to hire a New York outfit.

My choice was Pro Sports Inc., who, until I came along, had been involved for the most part with baseball, football and basketball players. But now the firm was to represent me and my teammates Walter Tkaczuk, Jean Ratelle and Vic Hadfield. Our advisors would be Marty Blackman and Steve Arnold, partners in the firm, and Paul Marcus, their assistant.

Although training camp wasn't set to open until September, we decided to meet early to plan our strategy before confronting Emile Francis. So on August 3 my father, brother and I gathered at the offices of Pro Sports to figure how we were going to get the money out of Emile Francis, whose nickname "The Cat" is not without reason.

To prepare me for Francis, Blackman sat behind the desk and played the part of The Cat. He'd give all sorts of reasons I shouldn't get much more money. "Why, you've only been in the league a year," he'd say. "It's too soon to tell how good you really are." Marty threw everything at me, and I listened carefully. But when the session was over,

I knew Marty was on my side, and at that point I was the highest-paid player in the history of the game.

We had no idea how Francis would react to Pro Sports representing me and, most of all, to the figure we were asking. I wondered, "Will The Cat say 'no' to me pleasantly, and smile, or will he throw me out of his office?" The more I thought about it, the more excited I became simply to see his reaction.

Trying to anticipate Francis became a game for me. I hoped he'd let me finish my salary pitch because I wanted him to be happy to give me what I wanted. A tough thing, making somebody happy to give you money.

Each day the drama mounted and the possibilities multiplied. I began thinking I'd turn out to be hockey's Curt Flood—I'd go all the way in arbitration, reject the final decision and then go to court. But this would be bad for me and bad for hockey; I didn't want that. So my first plan was to explain to The Cat that arbitration would not be in my favor. To be intelligent about all this, however, I had to sit down with my father and do some heavy talking.

Some people might consider it unusual for a 22-year-old professional athlete to bring his father into the middle of his contract negotiations. But that doesn't bother me. Right from the start I insisted he sit in on the meetings with Pro Sports Inc. There were several reasons for this. Most important was the fact that Dad had been present in 1968 when I signed my first contract with the Rangers.

"I want $10,000 to sign, and $17,500 to play in majors

or $12,500 to play in minors on a two-year contract," I'd told Francis at the time. And I meant it. The Cat objected, and we would have stalemated if my father hadn't said, "First, Brad, you have to prove yourself in this league before you make any outsized demands. Then you can come back here and tell Mr. Francis what you think you're worth." He turned to Emile and said, "If you could get a boy to play in the NHL for $10,000 it would be a steal, right? So why not give the lad a one-way contract at $10,000 for the first year, $10,000 for the second year and $5,000 to sign." Emile agreed to these figures; and I said I'd think about them.

Once home, I called Francis and told him I wanted $7,500 to sign. But we finally settled on $6,500 to sign, $10,000 the first year and $11,500 the second.

So I agreed to sign a two-year contract for $28,000. And I had discovered that Dad would not take my side in a dispute if he thought I was wrong. I took his advice then, and I still do, because he more than anybody else can put my pluses and minuses together.

Another thing I discovered in August 1970, was that the NHL owners did not want to face Brad Park in court and have to test the validity of the reserve clause.

On August 4 I had my first meeting with Francis. Before I went in I felt somewhat tense and a little afraid, not knowing quite what to expect. When I got to his office on the fourth floor of Madison Square Garden, the enemy was waiting. My opponents were The Cat and his assistant,

Denis Ball. I was accompanied by Marty Blackman, Steve Arnold and my father.

After the usual pleasantries, Marty fired the opening shot of what was to become a three-month war between The Cat and myself. Marty explained that even though his company represents, Jean, Vic, Walter and me, we are not to be handled as a package. Instead, each client tells Pro Sports what he wants, and discussions will then be held until an agreed-upon figure is obtained.

Marty told Francis that I was really disgusted when I got my first contract from him. He had offered me only $17,500 and I was damned mad. Marty then handed The Cat a typewritten piece of paper with my salary request on it.

Until then, Francis had been calm. But when he looked at the paper he exploded. "All right, fellas," he said. "I've shown you courtesy. Now, I'm fed up!" He went on to say that he didn't use the press when he conducted negotiations, and he was unhappy with what he considered "leaks" to newspapermen about the contract talks. I told him that whether what he said was true or not, it really had no bearing on what I wanted, because no newspaperman knew what I had asked for in terms of salary.

The Cat then jumped Steve and Marty, saying that Paul Marcus had approached him to offer Pro Sports' assistance in representing Francis. I was surprised to hear this; I couldn't figure out why Marcus would try to handle Francis.

At this point Steve popped up and said, "We represent

a lot of coaches and managers who do commercials for radio and TV. We handle people like Lombardi and Ewbank." Apparently The Cat didn't believe him, but we were getting bogged down in irrelevant matters. My father realized this and made it clear that he was also disappointed in Francis' contract offer. He reminded Francis of our original negotiations when I first turned pro, and that he'd gotten me for what amounted to a steal. They both agreed on that, and then my father recalled how Francis had said that if I proved myself I could come back and demand better money, just as we were now doing. We made it clear this wasn't a demand, but a request. Obviously, we hoped to keep discussions on a cool level.

I hadn't said a word yet, and I wasn't going to say one if I could help it. Things were going reasonable well; so button up, Brad.

Steve then asked Emile to justify his $17,500 offer. "If we took an average of the salaries being earned by NHL All-Stars—which Brad is—you'd find our request is not out of line," said Steve. "By the same token, if you consider the salaries made by such non–All-Stars as Tim Horton and Carl Brewer, you'd also find they're making one helluva sum. So again, by comparison, our request is not out of line."

Dad then made his move. He looked directly at Francis and said: "You once told Brad there were three things that count in a fellow's contract: his ability, his pull at the box office and his seniority. Brad has everything but seniority. Still, you'd admit he's going to get better as the

years go on, which is a plus for the Ranger organization."
He then compared me with two rookies, Gil Perreault of
Buffalo and Dale Tallon of Vancouver, and pointed out
that these inexperienced players were expecting $60,000
contracts, with expansion teams no less! "Brad has been
here two years," my father continued, "and in two years
he's done the same thing as Bobby Orr—he's made the
First All-Star Team. Now look at Brewer. He spent three
years in Finland, came back and is getting a big fat contract. Look what you're paying Horton. If you had to
choose between Horton and Brad, which one would you
rather have at Horton's salary?"

Emile shot back, "But Horton built it up over the
years."

My father quickly answered that he had a news clipping
quoting Francis as saying that I was to the Rangers what
Bobby Orr was to the Bruins. The Cat's offer, he con-
cluded, was far too low.

Now Steve contributed his two cents, reminding Francis
of my injury late in the 1969–70 season when the Rangers
were in first place, and recalling how the team had then
dropped down to fifth while I was out of the lineup. "The
injury was a terrible thing," Steve went on, "but it gave us
a chance to evaluate the team without Brad. Granted, no
one man wins hockey games, but Brad sure helps."

Finally, it was Marty's turn. He began by saying that
there are many players in the NHL who are journeymen
skaters who travel from team to team each year because
they're not really good enough to stay on with one club.

As Marty was talking I figured he was slowly going to build me up in Francis' estimation. But all of a sudden he said, "Brad is a superstar!" At which point the meeting rapidly came to an end. We presented our contract stipulations, thanked Emile for listening and left the office.

As we rode down in the elevator to the Garden's West 31st Street exit, I reflected on Francis' behavior. I'd been watching him throughout the discussion, trying to assess his reactions. Now, mulling them over in my mind, I realized there were actually few genuine responses I could put my finger on. Whenever something was said, Emile would seem to agree. He'd say, "Uh-huh, uh-huh . . ." like that. He wasn't happy and he wasn't angry—at least, not on the surface. He was just quiet, very quiet. Like a cobra waiting to strike. And when he strikes, I thought to myself, it's going to hurt.

Once we were outside again and walking up Eighth Avenue, I couldn't contain myself any longer. I was bothered about Paul Marcus suggesting to Francis that Pro Sports represent him.

"What kind of nonsense is this?" I said to them. "What happens if Steve represents Emile and Marty represents me. You two guys will be representing against each other —and you're in the same firm. You get 15 percent and you can't lose. Besides, I didn't know you guys represented Ewbank and Lombardi."

Steve came back with a great answer to that one. "Sure we do—Harry Lombardi and Charlie Ewbank!"

*   *   *

Day by day, little episodes occurred in August that led to a growing conflict between Francis and me. On August 5, Walter Tkaczuk, my closest friend, came to town to sit down with Francis and talk contract. Walter phoned me— I was out at the time—and told my wife that The Cat was pretty upset with him. When I heard the news I felt sorry for Walter because I know how it is to have a fellow like Emile mad at you. It makes you feel about two inches high. Then I got to wondering, "Why is he mad at Walter when he wasn't mad at me?" Very puzzling.

Soon after that Dad called to report that the newspapers were saying Dale Tallon had received a $60,000 contract from the new Vancouver Canucks. Imagine how I felt about that. This kid was just out of Junior hockey, was untried, was with an expansion team that didn't even know whether it would make money—and he was getting $60,000. Me, I'm with an established team that packs 17,250 into Madison Square Garden every game, I've proved myself an All-Star—and The Cat sends me a contract for $17,500. Besides that, I'm a better hockey player than Dale Tallon. I'll bet my life on it.

The news about Tallon doubled my determination to fight hard for a good contract. I decided to stick right to the end and, if necessary, I'd help my father sell insurance. At the same time, however, training camp was only a month away.

There's not much hockey in the New York papers during the summer, but one afternoon a reporter came to our hockey school in New Hyde Park and asked if I was looking forward to the new season. Actually I wasn't, though perhaps it was because I was worried about negotiations. Training camp is a lot of hard work. A year earlier it meant something because I had to prove I belonged in the NHL, that my first year wasn't a fluke and I wasn't going to suffer a sophomore jinx.

All of a sudden I realized there *was* something to prove in this, my third year. I had to prove that I was one of the two best defensemen in the league. Bobby Orr is first, and I won't argue that. But as far as second goes, I was going to have to beat out the rest of the NHL defensemen. Could I prove it? I thought I could. Because all I needed to do was convince myself. Once I did that, it would be easy to prove it to other people. All they had to do was watch me.

From the outset I knew I was dealing in a curious and very sensitive area in these contract negotiations with Francis. On the one hand we were enemies across the bargaining table; but, on the other, we were both working to finish first and to win the Stanley Cup.

One of the toughest things about this money dispute would be to stay friendly with Emile. At one point during the negotiations he might say I'm no good, that I'm this and I'm that. But after it's over, he might call me one of the best players in the world. Athletes have to understand this; sport is only a business and should be regarded as such (though it can also be great fun as well). Still, hockey is my living and the way I support my family, so these negotiations were of no little interest to me.

Otherwise, business was fine. The hockey school was going well, and I'd been approached to do a commercial for Wheaties breakfast cereal. Another interesting episode.

My previous contract stipulated that I owed the hockey club one-third of what I earned from any such commercial whenever I used the Ranger uniform. The other two-thirds was mine. I phoned Emile and asked if he'd take the third. He said he would, which meant the club would get a minimum of $1,100. Once he said that, I phoned Steve Arnold and told him about it. We decided to raise my contract request by $1,100.

Steve also said he'd met with Francis earlier in the day and The Cat had raised his original contract offer by $10,000—$27,500 for one year, or $30,000 a year on a two-year contract. "Since Emile has come up $10,000," Steve humorously suggested, "let's back off $10,000."

"Heck no," I told Steve. "We'll go down $8,900. I want my $1,100."

By mid-August we'd reached a quiet period. There were no exchanges between Pro Sports and the Rangers' front office. The final week of the month I began getting in shape for training camp. I skated every day trying to take off ten pounds. For me it's hard since I put on weight easily and shed it with difficulty.

But I wasn't the only player with problems. Wherever I turned, it seemed a friend of mine was up to his neck.

One was Terry Caffrey, a buddy from early Toronto hockey days. He belonged to the Chicago Black Hawks and had had a good season the previous year—something like 42 points in 40 games—until he was sidelined with torn knee ligaments. Now the Black Hawks hadn't even invited him to their camp. Instead, they wanted him to report to their minor-league training base.

This bothered me as much as it did Caffrey because I know he's one of the best centers in the Chicago organization. I told him that if I was in his shoes I wouldn't even report to the minor-league camp, as he belonged on the shores of Lake Michigan.

Another guy with problems was my teammate Vic Hadfield, who's also represented by Pro Sports. He had just been offered a terrific job by the Spalding sports equipment company, which wanted him to be their U.S. representative; a lifetime job at a generous salary. Vic had to choose between this offer and hockey. The fellows at Pro Sports thought Vic would be smarter taking the Spalding job because the pay is better than what the Rangers offered and he wouldn't have to knock his brains out.

But I know deep down that Vic will choose to play hockey because he not only plays it for the money—which, sometimes, isn't that great—but because he loves the game. And I'd make the same choice, because every Canadian boy grows up dreaming of playing in the NHL. Mark my words: Vic will return to the Rangers rather than go with Spalding!

One happy note. Walter Tkaczuk has decided to go to

Vic Tanny's health studio to build up his chest. That's like a Sherman tank adding a bulldozer, because Walt is one of the strongest men in the league. He skates over opponents instead of around them. But Walter told me he wanted to strengthen himself even more and that he's also going to take boxing lessons. My advice to all those who want to tangle with him is that you can be my guest. I'm going to put Walt in front of me whenever I get into a scrap.

Another interesting bit of news developed in Toronto. Dave Keon, the Toronto Maple Leafs' captain, has demanded a $125,000 contract for the new season, and if he doesn't get it, he won't play for the Leafs.

Dave's kid brother, Jimmy, is a pal of mine, and Jimmy told me Dave is a little upset because he's afraid his teammates will become annoyed about his salary demand. I told Jimmy I wouldn't hold it against any of my teammates if they managed a big salary because that, in turn, helps the other fellows. Big salaries are what the NHL needs. If one fellow on one team receives a large salary, then everyone else on the team can come in and ask for substantial raises. Eventually, hockey salaries may reach the level of basketball, football and baseball salaries. And that's why I think my holdout is good for hockey. The average salary in our game is something like $16,000, whereas in baseball, football and basketball it's about $25,000. When you consider we play many more games than football players and that our sport is much rougher than basketball and baseball, it's obvious that, all things being equal, hockey players are drastically underpaid.

Apparently, Emile Francis did not agree. On August 31 I received a registered letter from him, instructing me that he had decided "in the best interests of the New York Rangers" we should go to arbitration to settle my contract dispute.

This I did not like at all. I knew arbitration was not going to help me because the arbitrator would give me only a small raise over my last salary. Hence I didn't want to go to arbitration, and I made up my mind then and there to fight it.

How the war between myself (not to mention Vic, Walter, and Jean) and the Rangers mushroomed can be understood from the following exchange of letters, starting with The Cat's missive to me:

August 24, 1970

Dear Brad,

The purpose of this letter is to advise you that due to the impasse we have now reached in contract negotiations, and in accordance with the owner-players' council agreement, I am, on behalf of the New York Rangers, Inc., requesting arbitration.

As you are well aware of, any unsigned protected player whose contract has not been signed by August 20th then proceeds to arbitration.

In order to follow the intent of the agreement, I am prepared to discuss with you the identity of the arbitrator, whom we both must mutually agree to.

Looking forward to hearing from you at your earliest convenience, I remain

> Sincerely,
> New York Rangers, Inc.
> Emile Francis
> Vice President and General Manager

Copies of this letter were sent to Clarence Campbell, President of the National Hockey League; Alan Eagleson, Executive Director NHL Players' Association; Charles Mulcahy.

Pro Sports answer to Emile's letter read as follows:

August 27, 1970

Dear Emile,

We have received copies of your letters of August 24th, directed to Vic Hadfield, Brad Park, Walter Tkaczuk, and Jean Ratelle. For reasons stated in our last meeting, we are not prepared to recommend arbitration to any of our clients. Arbitration may have its value in a free economy, where individuals can seek competitive offers for their services. Obviously, due to the reserve clause, players are restricted in this regard.

We are willing to recommend arbitration in the event we are unable to obtain better competitive terms for our clients' services than your last offers. To seek competitive offers would necessitate your notifying all NHL clubs that they are free to negotiate for the services of our clients, and should an arrangement be consummated, you would release them.

Should you not be prepared to take the above-stated course of action, we must stand firm in refusing to submit the matter to arbitration.

On the other hand, we are ready and willing to continue to

negotiate in good faith with you in an attempt to reach a mutually acceptable compromise agreement for each of our players. We hope that you agree that continued negotiations will make the matter of arbitration academic, and look forward to your response.

Sincerely,

R. Steven Arnold

Copies of this letter were sent to Walter Tkaczuk, Jean Ratelle, Brad Park, Vic Hadfield, and Alan Eagleson.

Emile responded:

August 31, 1970

Dear Steve,

In reply to your letter of August 27th, we hereby advise you that if your clients, Messrs. Hadfield, Ratelle, Park, Tkaczuk refuse to submit their salary disputes to arbitration, they will be in violation of the terms of their employment contracts, and also of the agreements between the National Hockey League and the National Hockey League Players' Association.

Persuant to such contracts and agreements, either the club or the player has the right, after August 20, to submit salary disputes to arbitration, provided both parties agree upon an arbitrator, or arbitrators.

Accordingly, we repeat our demand for arbitration and suggest that the arbitrator or arbitrators be either and/or both of Clarence S. Campbell or Alan Eagleson.

Sincerely,

New York Rangers, Inc.

Emile Francis

Vice President and General Manager

Copies of this letter were sent to Clarence Campbell, Charles Mulcahy, Alan Eagelson, Vic Hadfield, Brad Park, Jean Ratelle, Walter Tkaczuk.

Offhand, arbitration might seem the best solution in my case because it's so often used to settle labor disputes. But arbitration in the NHL is a completely different matter, very unfair to players.

Here's why. When The Cat suggested that Clarence Campbell and Alan Eagleson be the arbitrators, I naturally objected. As League president, Campbell is paid by the owners and, therefore, will be on the owners' side in any dispute such as mine. As for Eagleson, although he is the advisor to the NHL Players' Association, he's also a rival of Pro Sports, my negotiators. And since he's their competitor, it follows that he's *my* competitor. Therefore, neither Campbell nor Eagleson were suitable to me as arbitrators.

Knowing this, I showed up at the Rangers' training camp in Kitchener, Ontario, on September 10. I'd been told early in our negotiating battle that I'd probably suffer a few sleepless nights, but I hadn't had one all summer. Suddenly, the night before camp opened, I couldn't get to sleep. Two things were bothering me—my contract and my weight, which wasn't going to be 196 pounds, where I'd wanted it for the opening of camp. I had eaten too much during the summer and I weighed 200 pounds—a butterball.

Meanwhile, I realized The Cat and I were at an impasse.

And try as I might, I couldn't help but wonder and worry a bit about what he'd do next.

The opening days of training camp are always pleasant because you meet a lot of the guys you haven't seen for some time and also get to pal with some of the minor-league players you knew from other years and other teams. One of my favorite people is Forbes Kennedy. Forbsie was at the 1970 Rangers' camp, although he wasn't expected to make the New York club. He's a little guy with a big sense of humor who never stops putting people on.

The first day of camp the doctors were giving us the usual physical tests and Forbes was passing water in the washroom for his urine sample. Forbsie is so small that when he sits on the bench in the dressing room his skates don't even touch the floor. So now the doctor calls in from the other room, "Forbes, how tall are you?"

There was a pause, and with both rooms quiet, Forbes yelled back, "Six-two!"

After completing our tests, I drove to the nearby hospital with my teammate, Arnie Brown, for the chest X ray. Yet even though this is required on the first day of camp, a sad accident occurred opening morning in September 1968, when I was a rookie.

One of the fellows then in camp was a tough forward from Winnipeg, Wayne Larkin. He'd been around the minors for a few years and was getting what appeared to be his last really good shot at an NHL berth. Larkin was among a bunch of players out on the ice for an early skate when, all of a sudden, he collapsed in a corner of the rink.

Bernie Geoffrion, our coach at the time, leaped over the boards and tried to revive poor Wayne by artificial respiration. Finally, somebody found a doctor, who tried pounding Larkin's chest to get his heart working again. I'll never forget the sight of Wayne stretched out on the ice, the guys around him and the ambulance coming in through the rear entrance, backing up on the ice and at last taking him to the hospital. It was too late, though, because Wayne had already died of a heart attack. And this on the first morning of my first day at training camp.

On September 11 skating began in earnest. Larry Popein, a former Ranger center who is now coaching our farm team in Seattle, put us through a drill so tough I bet one of the guys that "Pope" would never run out of exercises. And I won my bet. He just kept us going for the whole hour and a half, by which time I'd had it.

The second day Francis took over. He gave us a few drills and a light skate in the morning, and surprised us with a scrimmage in the afternoon. Guess what? I scored the first goal of training camp. So things were looking good. I knew I was a little heavy; still, I was skating and moving the puck well, and I felt good. But when I got off the ice, there was a message to see Emile at 8:30 that evening in his room at our motel. Immediately I talked to my buddies. Vic, it turned out, was supposed to see him at 7:30, Walter at 8:00 and Jean at 9:00. None of us had signed, and none of us knew what The Cat had up his sleeve.

Francis was playing a waiting game. That was obvious. And it was clear he'd made his last offer, and now just wanted the four of us to go to arbitration and get it over with. Our meeting produced no results.

"Emile," I said, "I didn't want Eagleson to negotiate my contract, so I sure as heck don't want him to arbitrate it."

The Cat retorted, "Well, we've got to find somebody who knows what's going on, who knows NHL salaries." I asked him who he'd recommend. He couldn't think of anybody, so we said good-night. Nothing. But that didn't affect my work in scrimmages. The next morning I scored a goal for my folks, who'd driven over from Toronto to watch us, and got two assists in the afternoon. Still, my weight was bugging me: 197 in the morning, and at the end of the day, after two workouts, 197 again!

Meanwhile, Francis escalated the war one notch. He banned Steve and Marty from the rink. I thought it a stupid move on The Cat's part because it's of no consequence whether they watch the workouts or not. They don't bother anybody. They just want to watch like anyone else.

As if that wasn't enough, the next morning my weight had jumped to 198, so I decided to wear a weight-reducing sweat jacket during the afternoon scrimmage. Then in the morning shift I pulled my groin, something I hadn't done since I was a kid. And I began thinking that maybe I wasn't in such good shape after all.

I told The Cat I had pulled my groin, and if he thought

I was slacking off, that was why. He said, "Well, nobody is going to slack it in my outfit!" With that I knew I'd have to bust my ass just the same—and with a bad groin to boot. I tried to joke with Emile, and told him the reason I pulled my groin was because I was a lot faster this year and couldn't adjust to my new speed. I don't recall him laughing.

Later that day, the heat between Francis and the four holdouts got a bit warmer. Pro Sports sent a letter to Emile informing him that we were not going to play in any of the exhibition games. If Francis wanted us to stay around, fine, we'd work out with the club maybe another week. We decided definitely, however, to walk out before the end of the training camp because we had to force The Cat to make a move. At that point he was just sitting back and waiting. And personally, this waiting game was getting to me, so we had to do something to shake up the status quo. A walkout seemed best. The first showdown was to occur Thursday night when the club was scheduled to play Buffalo in Peterborough, Ontario. Then it was back to Kitchener for a Friday game against St. Louis, and then on to New York for a game Sunday.

By this time there was no doubt The Cat knew I was working on a book. In fact, he cornered me after the first workout and laid down the law that I'd have to clear any endorsements through his office. It is in my old contract, but I'd forgotten about it so I had to inform him about a small record I was making and about my endorsing Adirondack's Sher-Wood hockey stick, not to mention this book.

He specifically asked to read the manuscript, though I told him I wasn't going to make him sound like a bad man. And actually, he's not.

Apart from the agonizing effect the holdout was having on me and my family, I was concerned about the reaction it might have on my teammates. To settle this matter I visited defenseman Rod Seiling and right wing Rod Gilbert, two veteran Rangers and particular friends of mine. I told them I was having problems with The Cat and was worrying about what the other fellows would think if I got a big salary, or if I decided not to play and missed the exhibition games because of my dispute.

"Don't worry," Gilbert said. "And do what *you* think is best. Nobody on the team will hold anything against you. They'll be happy to see you get a lot of money because it will help many of them." I really appreciated those words.

One by one reports would filter into camp about players on other teams. Even though I realized I should be primarily concerned with myself, I couldn't help wondering when I read the Toronto Maple Leafs were going to pay Mike Walton $40,000, and he was a fellow who'd played for them the past two years when the club didn't even make the playoffs—and the previous year they'd finished in last place. So here I was with New York: We'd made the playoffs twice in those years, and The Cat wouldn't go any higher than $30,000. That was pretty hard to comprehend, and it made me wonder whether I was dumb or whether I was approaching this business the wrong way. Emile had become more hardened in his attitude. He'd refused to confer with Pro Sports anymore and insisted on arbitration. "I'm tired of being penpals," he said.

Emile certainly had a sense of humor. But I was dead serious. I'd decided not to play in the exhibition games, because if I got hurt during those games I'd have to accept what I made a year ago or the last offer made by the club. It didn't make sense to take a chance.

My weight continued to confuse me. On September 15 I weighed in at 197 and weighed out at 193. I was so pleased I celebrated by having an enormous Chinese dinner. I realize Chinese food can be a great thing for putting on weight, but with only one life to live I might as well live it in all my glory!

Our training camp routine never varied: rise at 7:30 A.M., drive to the rink, suit up in time to be on the ice at 8:30 A.M., then scrimmage until 10 A.M. Drive to Minnie's Kitchen for a breakfast of soup, milk and maybe a Pepsi or two, because I'm usually pretty thirsty. Back to the motel for a nap, then back to the rink for a second workout from 1:30 to 2:30 P.M.

For laughs I sometimes play golf. One afternoon, following the workout, I played with Bobby Nevin (our captain), Dave Balon and Syl Apps. A few days earlier Syl and I were partners and we beat Nevin and Balon for $3.50 each. So they demanded a rematch, and this time we beat them for $4.75. That's a meal.

At this time of year a lot of bantering goes on. During a workout I hit Syl with one of the best bodychecks I'd ever thrown. In fact, I hit him so hard I began thinking about it later on in the day until I was really quite upset. So when I saw Syl that evening I said straight out, "Syl, I'm sorry I hit you at center."

"When?" he asked. And gave me one of those blank Jack Benny looks. Well, whether Syl was kidding or not, his reaction got through to me and I decided to be more aggressive. This would keep the guys off me and give me more room to handle the puck and see what's going on.

That night our dispute escalated another notch. The four of us met The Cat and told him we were serious about missing the exhibition games. Emile said we'd be breaking the contract we'd signed, and insisted we were obligated to play the exhibitions. I told him he was wrong: If we were on a continuous contract—which we weren't— it might be true. But since we were unsigned we weren't even obligated to report to camp, let alone play exhibitions. He didn't argue the point, so I guess I was right. Our first exhibition game was scheduled for the next night, and we all were wondering what The Cat would do.

II

Suspension

Since our position was now firmly established, Emile had to set up two schedules, one for the rest of the team and one for the holdouts. We figured that working out with the Buffalo and Omaha farm teams would keep us in shape. For whatever transpired, we wanted to be fit when we returned to the team at the start of the season. And this we all still expected to do.

That night Francis showed the team a film, called *Second Effort*. It featured football's late Vince Lombardi, and the message was clear—dedication to one's team and one's job will produce results. I learned from the film that by trying harder I'd improve and would eventually make more money at my profession. But I've already proven myself, and I feel I'm entitled to a larger salary now. I truly believe I have a lot of ability, and I don't think the Rangers' offer came close to what I deserve.

At 12:45 P.M. on the afternoon of September 17, 1970, I was officially suspended by the New York Rangers. Here

I was in only my third NHL season, and suspended! It makes a man think.

My first thoughts zeroed right in on Francis and his motives. To me it seemed an act of revenge. My feelings were reinforced after a meeting with him. He said I'd broken two clauses in my contract: one when I wouldn't go to arbitration and the second when I wouldn't play in exhibition games.

Both allegations were absolutely untrue.

We had never decided on an arbitrator, which eliminates point one. And I was not obliged to report to camp unsigned, *let alone* play in exhibition games unsigned, which destroys point two. I told The Cat what I thought, said good-bye, packed my bags and drove to my folks' home in Toronto. If there was a bright spot in the entire episode it was that my wife, Gerry, had just returned to Toronto after visiting her parents in Winnipeg. Seeing her was just the tonic I needed, because no man enjoys being suspended—and unfairly so—from his livelihood.

Too, I'd primed myself mentally for training camp as well as the exhibition schedule. And now this disruption. If nothing else, however, I now had a chance to reflect on what had happened up until then; on our team, on the opposition and on the future.

As a Ranger, you inevitably get to thinking about the Boston Bruins, because they are the team we must beat to finish first and win the Stanley Cup. I remember one night when I was still playing and we had an exhibition with the Bruins. Francis said he wanted a tight game.

With the score 6–6 in the third period, our goalie, Ed Giacomin, cracked, "Well, Emile's got his tight game!"

Boston eventually won 8–6, and on the plane home that night the stewardesses introduced themselves over the loud-speaker. "This is Mrs. Bucyk," said one. And then, "This is Miss Cheevers and Miss Green." It just seemed that everywhere we went the Bruins were hounding us.

Our trouble with Boston began right in training camp. Or maybe it was a carryover from the previous spring when we had that bloody awful playoff with them. Whatever it was, in that early exhibition Phil Esposito took several potshots at me, which I didn't like.

Why did he do it? I know. I like to take him into the boards, which upsets him. A lot of people don't realize it, but Esposito gets annoyed—more than the average player —when he's taken out of a play. Maybe he thinks he's too good to be touched. Whatever it is, he once retaliated against me with a hard slash on my left elbow which raised a considerable lump.

What Esposito did to me, however, is a classic example of hockey's "in-fighting," and it's important for the player who's hit to even things up eventually or else the other guy will start taking liberties that could make life miserable for him. So I made up my mind then and there that I was going to take a dandy cut at Esposito to get my revenge. I'm like an elephant: I don't forget who hits me. I'll even-tually line him up and give him an extra shot.

*   *   *

By the second day of the suspension I began to appreciate what loneliness is all about. At home I'd sit around
and play solitaire because that game gives me a good opportunity to think as I don't have to concentrate on the
cards. Golf is my other diversion but, much as I enjoy it,
golf only entertains me so much and that's that.

The solitude was finally broken on September 19 when
Bob Pennington, a columnist for the Toronto *Telegram,*
came to visit me. He asked how far apart I was from
Francis, what the Rangers were offering and what I wanted.
Legitimate questions, except I didn't feel free to answer
them. And for the first time I realized that Francis and I
hadn't argued, we hadn't negotiated, and we were still
miles apart.

We—which, of course, includes Vic, Jean and Walter—
realized that people like Bob Pennington weren't really
familiar with the problems behind our holdout, so Pro
Sports decided to hold a press conference in Toronto to
spell out our position clearly. We were in a somewhat
awkward position because it appeared the four of us were
banded together, which was not the case. But, for his own
crafty purposes, Francis had lumped us together to make
it *appear* we were sandbagging him. Hopefully the press
conference would clear the air a bit. As the subject of a
press conference, I wondered what it would be like.

I was amused to see that the Rangers played an exhibition against Buffalo, a brand new expansion team, and
fell behind 0–4 before they rallied to tie the game 4–4
in the last 28 seconds. While such an inept performance

makes the four of us look good, I still hope my friends on the team will do well. Yet I want them to miss me.

I've also been keeping a careful eye on some of the lesser players. One is Don Blackburn, a forward, who banged around the minors for a while and played briefly with Philadelphia. He's not flashy, but he works hard and never gets caught out of position.

Then there's Pierre Jarry, a French-Canadian boy with a lot of promise. Unlike Blackburn, who goes about 200 pounds, Jarry must be under 170, and his unpleasant chore is guarding Blackburn in the scrimmages. Every workout Jarry takes a run at Blackburn, hits him and just bounces off. What's amazing about little Pierre is that he's played the entire training period with a pulled groin, and yet he still takes runs at people and outraces a lot of the veterans. Once he was so tired he lagged behind and Francis, who was on the touchy side, threw him off the ice. Pierre started arguing, which is a bad thing to do with The Cat, and Francis just waved him off. Jarry left the rink almost in tears.

The press conference was held on Monday afternoon, September 21 at Toronto's biggest hotel, The Royal York. At first, Pro Sports considered holding it in New York City because we do play for the Rangers, but it was decided that Toronto would be a better site since training camp was only an hour's drive, at Kitchener, and Toronto was more interested in hockey in September than New York.

Prior to our meeting with the media, we gathered at my

house for a briefing on what had developed and what strategy Francis would probably take in the days to come. The only conclusion reached was that our suspension meant very little beyond the fact that the club had asked us to leave camp and was using this as a tactical ploy against us in negotiations. Sometimes this bickering got a bit over my head, and that's where I let Pro Sports take over.

The press conference was exciting but frustrating. The room was crowded, and everyone fired away with the usual questions about what we were asking and how far we were prepared to go. We had to take the same nebulous position because no real bargaining had taken place with Francis. The only satisfaction of the whole day was news that the Red Wings beat the Rangers 5–2, and our club looked awful.

It's strange. When I was a kid I read in the papers about hockey players having contract troubles and holding out, and I never understood what was going on. Now I'm right in the middle of the scene and everything has crystallized and it's *still* hard to comprehend.

What makes it so incomprehensible is the fact that everybody knows—I know, Francis knows, Pro Sports knows, the players know, the public knows—that in the end I'll get more money to play hockey for New York. The only question is how much, and I figure it's a waste of time for Francis to go through all the nonsense, which isn't helping him, not helping me and not helping the team. It's all a big game and a silly one at that, and sitting around doing nothing drives me nuts.

Come to think of it, though, that's exactly what Francis may be trying to do—drive me nuts—on the assumption that the pressure will soon get the best of me and I'll give in and come around to sign for something approximating their terms. But I'm wise to that. I simply keep busy and take my mind off the negotiations.

So on Tuesday night, September 22, I went over to Maple Leaf Gardens and skated with Joe Kane and the Orillia Terriers. Kane is a Toronto attorney who also is a hockey nut. For a while he was president of the Central Pro League, but then he returned to Toronto where he's now practicing law. The Terriers are a senior-league team from a community not far north of Toronto, and the workout was good for me.

The next morning Kane phoned. "Sorry, Brad," he said, "but you can't work out with us anymore. Francis won't let you." Something to do with an agreement between the Canadian Amateur Hockey Association and the NHL to keep suspended players like me from working out with any CAHA-affiliated teams like the Terriers.

That burned me. All I was doing was trying to keep in shape so that when I signed I'd be ready for the Rangers. I was doing Francis a favor. But, obviously, he plans to put the screws into me however he can. And he is.

Wednesday, September 23, I finally met head-to-head with Francis and got absolutely nowhere. Marty Blackman and Steve Arnold were with me. I wanted to know why I didn't deserve the money I'd requested—or anything even close to what I'd asked for.

"My last offer," said Francis, "is $27,500 for one year, or $30,000 apiece for two years. That's all you're worth! Not a penny more. Anything else you'll have to get through arbitration."

My insides were boiling, but I had vowed to stay cool. "You must have your reasons," I said. "And I'm entitled to hear them."

Francis took over. "You've been two years in the league and you've made the All-Stars. But other players who have higher salaries have earned them. They've been consistent for six or seven years. You haven't been around that long, so you don't deserve what they're getting. My $30,000 offer is fair. If you don't take it you're out of your mind."

"Emile, I don't think it is fair," I said. "A rookie like Dale Tallon is getting $60,000 and he hasn't even stepped on NHL ice." Francis counterattacked. His argument was that Tallon would be playing for Vancouver, and in order to give hockey a splash in the new NHL city, the Canucks decided to give him big money.

As the bickering went on I had the urge to get up and do something irrational, like belt Francis in the mouth, but I didn't. "Emile," I continued, "what more can I tell you? I think I deserve what I'm asking. You don't. There's nothing else I can say except that you're a cheap s.o.b."

Then Steve and Marty got into the act, talking about the legal end of things. They questioned Francis' idiotic move of taking away our skates. Imagine Vic, Jean, Walt and me with our blades confiscated, so if we wanted to do a bit of skating to stay in condition, we didn't even have skates.

"Well," said Francis, "the skates belong to the club."
Brilliant. What bearing has that on our contract problems?
Nothing, except it shows he'll go to any limit to give us
the business.

He explained why he wouldn't let me work out with
Joe Kane and the Orillia team. "It's part of the NHL–
CAHA agreement. It can't be bent or broken. You don't
bend or break a contract; you stick to it."

By now I was convinced Francis was carrying his ven-
detta too far. Nothing was gained by the meeting. It was
a waste of time, except to give me an insight into his thinking. He inspired me to stick to my guns. I want to play
hockey, but there is just no talking to him at the moment.
That unspeakable Cat really has my fur up.

The same night the Rangers played an exhibition game
against Boston. It was terrible. New York blew a 2–0 lead
and the Ranger defense was full of holes; particularly since
the Bruins weren't even playing Bobby Orr, Phil Esposito,
Derek Sanderson, Johnny Bucyk or Ed Westfall. It's obvious the Rangers missed us. Also, Arnie Brown has a bad
knee and left for New York to have it examined, and
Jimmy Neilson's knee isn't right.

The Bruins' defense, I noticed, is nothing without Orr.
He gets the puck out for them and shows them what to do
with it. They did play Teddy Green, but he just didn't
seem to have it. He was making bad passes, wasn't reacting
with that split-second timing you need in the NHL and
the fans were needling him. During the game one of them
shouted, "What's the matter, Green, is that plate in your

head too heavy for you?" A man has to be a jackass to make a crack like that. Still, it's obvious Green hasn't fully recovered from his skull fracture, and I feel sorry for him. But I also give him credit for trying a comeback.

I returned home after the game and talked with my father. He made a good point. The reason Francis suspended us was because we refused to play in an exhibition game. What if we made it clear—perhaps through the press—that we'd now be willing to play? Would he lift the suspension? I wonder.

Without my knowledge, Dad decided on Thursday, September 24, to meet privately with The Cat. When he arrived home at two o'clock the next morning and told me what had happened, it was a real shocker!

Francis had agreed to submit the contract deadlock to two arbitrators. One would be NHL President Clarence Campbell, who has often handled arbitration. And the other, believe it or not, would be my father.

"How do you feel about that?" Dad asked.

"Let's go to Kitchener tomorrow and talk about it with The Cat," I said.

It was 2:30 A.M. when I went to bed, but I couldn't fall asleep. I thought and thought and tried to puzzle things out in my mind. Finally I decided to go along with my father. I think he has an accurate idea of what I'm worth.

The next morning I drove to Kitchener and consulted with Francis. We agreed on the two arbitrators, but I was unhappy when I left his office because he continued to attack Pro Sports Inc. in a transparent attempt to cause dissension in the ranks. I told him straight out that Pro Sports was and would continue to be my advisor. I lost a bit by going to see Francis, but I still have my pride.

After leaving Francis I rejoined the team. Ab DeMarco, whom I've known for quite a long time, walked up as if he'd never seen me before and introduced himself. He then offered to introduce me to all the fellows.

"By the way," asked DeMarco. "Who are you and what are you doing here?"

"My name is Brad Park," I repeated, "and I'm the guy who's going to take your job away from you."

Just then my buddy Syl Apps joined us and asked why I'd come back. "I ran out of meal money," I said. The guys laughed, and I felt happy again.

Out on the ice everything felt perfectly normal for the first ten minutes or so. Then, during a scrimmage, the gut pains began knifing through my body, coming and going every few minutes. Somewhat desperately, I tried not to give in to them. But then Francis sent us through the post-scrimmage skate, and my legs felt riveted to the ice. Just lifting them became a monumental job. My stamina was gone, and I felt I'd collapse any second. Yet somehow I lasted until the end. But as the guys trooped off, Francis called me aside. "I want you to do some wind sprints," he ordered.

There was no choice. Back and forth I labored, digging my toes into the ice, pulling together whatever energy I had left and growing sicker by the second. At last he let me go to the dressing room. I headed straight for the toilet bowl.

I had explained my position to Walter Tkaczuk and to Pro Sports, and that night Walt returned to camp. He told me that he'd gotten a Kitchener lawyer to represent him in the arbitration with Campbell.

The same night I drove to the Kitchener rink with a fellow named Barry Thompson who had come all the way from Saskatoon, Saskatchewan, to try out as a goaltender with one of the Rangers' farm teams. He'd taken time off from his job with hopes of making it in pro hockey.

"They just told me to go back home," Thompson said. "I guess I'm not good enough. 'Don't call us, we'll call you,' they said."

I felt miserable listening to Thompson. Here I was getting set to return to the NHL and this other guy had just been told he wasn't good enough. I tried to cheer him but there was no way. He'd come to camp and done his best, and now he had to drive back across Canada to his job in Saskatoon.

"What do you do?" I asked hopefully.

He looked at me sadly. "I'm a milkman," he said.

I wonder whether he really did get a good look at camp or whether, maybe, our brain trusts just might have missed out on a prospect who should have been sent to an Eastern League team like the Long Island Ducks. Once a long time ago a guy everybody had overlooked wound up in Long Island, and he eventually became an All-Star: Eddie Giacomin.

The waiting game continues over the contracts. The

four of us are back in camp and we're going through the routine. One day our old coach Bernie Geoffrion, who's now scouting for the Rangers, dropped around, and somebody mentioned to him that Frank Mahovlich of Detroit said he thought he could score 50 goals this year.

The Boomer is a very proud man, especially proud that he is one of the very few people in NHL history to have scored 50 goals in a season. "Listen," said Geoffrion, "it's easy to score 50 goals in the paper, but it's not so easy to score dem on da hice!"

Tuesday, September 29, Francis put us to a test. He ordered the four holdouts to dress and play against the Red Wings. Since our playing return was one of the provisions we made to get the arbitrators we wanted, there was no choice but to agree. We did, and we beat Detroit 4–3. I played well, which was important, but not as important as the meeting between Campbell and my father set for the next day.

Our club looks solid. There are plenty of young kids around who could make the team but won't because of our depth. Ab DeMarco is one. He's a defenseman who can handle the puck well and has a good head. His problem is weight. He only weighs 165 pounds, and when he goes into the corners he gets pushed off the puck. Tom Miller, a big young center, is another prospect who won't make the club because we have Ratelle, Tkaczuk and Apps. And there are also others who will be heading off to various minor-league teams when camp breaks on Wednesday, September 30.

The close of training camp is always sad. When the

players disband, a lot of friendships inevitably end, sometimes never to be renewed. Forbes Kennedy is one. When he walked out of the motel I shouted to him, "See you later, Forbsie. Try and have a good year."

But deep down I know that because of his leg problems he doesn't have a chance. Forbsie doesn't even know where he's going, yet there he was with his skates hanging over his shoulder, the plug of a cigar jammed in his mouth and a smile on his face. Maybe he didn't even know he was washed up.

That night I drove from Kitchener to New York City and arrived at 3:30 Thursday morning. Francis had us out practicing Friday for our exhibition game in St. Louis on Saturday. Later in the afternoon I drove to the airport with Eddie Giacomin, Arnie Brown, Syl Apps and my wife. As I drove along the Van Wyck Expressway toward LaGuardia Airport, I began thinking how all these sights were once so new and exciting to me when I was a rookie and how they must now be exciting to Syl. I wanted to ask Syl what he was thinking, but somehow I never got it out.

Saturday afternoon before our night hockey game, a bunch of us watched the televised National Baseball League playoff between Pittsburgh and Cincinnati. The umpires were on strike, and Emile Francis said that he had once been active in baseball and maybe he'd volunteer to ump in the World Series. "That's great, Emile," I told him. "You're so small you won't even have to crouch to look over the catcher." Soon the other guys picked up my needling of Francis about his size. Eddie Giacomin asked

Emile if he had any extra Ranger team jackets. And Francis said he had a couple of his own he hadn't even worn.

"I'd like them for my kids," said Giacomin, "and yours ought to fit 'em!"

Emile took it all in good humor. I figured the reason must be that he'd just signed somebody to a contract—on *his* terms. Francis was even in good spirits after the game, which we just squeeked out, 6–5, even though we played poorly. I suffered a charley horse and was sitting on the bench with an ice pack on my leg. Apparently Emile remembered our needling him earlier, because he walked over and said to me, "Whatsa matter, one of the fans throw a program that hit you in the leg?"

Somehow, the way he said it made me forget all the problems I'd been having with him, and I could only think what a great guy Emile really is. Even if I don't get the money I want.

Following the game we returned to New York. And on Monday afternoon I spoke with Francis. He told me the arbitration between my father and Campbell was off. When I telephoned Dad, he said that Campbell had been rude to him in their discussions, and he was fed up with the whole thing. Only a few days left before the season starts, and we're still nowhere.

After I hung up, my wife Gerry walked into the room and mentioned, "Y'know, Brad, once you sign your contract I'm going to buy some material and make curtains."

Now there's optimism. She made the contract settlement sound like tomorrow.

Well, tomorrow came, and it was bleak. Francis said we'd gone the route. "I'm going to give you a few days to think about it," he said. "I've made my last offer. You can have until Friday to decide whether to accept it or not. If you don't, we'll start deducting from your salary on Saturday when the season starts. There will be a deduction for every day you miss."

I told him I knew all about that and I wasn't going to accept his offer now or on Friday. He led me to believe the higher-ups in Madison Square Garden laid down the limits of my contract. So I went over to the office of Pro Sports, where it was decided to wait until Friday before making any new moves. Everyone seemed to feel management might make a new offer by then, because Francis had upped his offer to Ratelle and Ratty was near signing. I know Jean is a sensitive guy and I knew he'd be wondering whether he'd let us down if he signed first. So I phoned him and said, "Y'know, Jean, if you get what you want, don't worry about the rest of us. Go right ahead and sign."

Our next exhibition game was scheduled for Boston, and when we arrived at Logan Airport, the bus was waiting for us as usual. There was only one difficulty: The driver was a new man who had never gone from the airport to the hotel. Well, he was something. He kept winding up on bridges where the super structure was so low the bus didn't have clearance. Then he'd have to back off and find another way. "Take a run at it," yelled Giacomin. Then each guy tried a line. "Let the air out of the tires," said Ron Stewart, "and try to squeeze under."

Somebody else called out, "Put the Italian [Eddie Giacomin] on top. He's covered with olive oil so we'll slip right through!" The bus driver was really rattled by this time. And when he finally did make it to the toll station at the tunnel, there we were in the line marked "CARS ONLY —EXACT CHANGE."

If that wasn't enough to squirrel the night, when I got to my hotel room and turned on the television there was Derek Sanderson, Mr. Wise-Guy of the Bruins. As usual, his comments made me sick. He said athletes are overpaid and overrated. "It may hurt my contract negotiations," he said, "but that's the way I feel."

"Screw you," I said and turned off the set.

That, more or less, was my feeling toward Francis as the week came to an end and we returned to New York. Jean and Vic broke the ice by signing just before the team left for the opening game in St. Louis. But Walter and I remained unhappy, and on October 10 we watched the fellows leave for the airport to fly to St. Louis.

There had been one final attempt to break the impasse late in the week. "What do you want?" Francis had asked me. "Let's get it on the table." When I told him, he replied, "That's fine, but my offer still goes and I'm obligated to stick with it because it's what Clarence Campbell believes is fair and Campbell is a knowledgeable hockey man."

Campbell, as everyone knows, works for the owners. They pay his salary. "Emile," I told him, "if that's what Campbell thinks I deserve, then I have no respect for his judgment or what he thinks!"

"Then we're still stuck in the mud," he said.

I agreed, with one small addition. *"Deep* in the mud," I replied.

"Where do we go from here?" Emile asked.

"Well," I answered, "you go to St. Louis and I go home to watch the game on TV."

Walter and I agreed The Cat was playing a waiting game with us. We believed he reasoned this way: Park and Tkaczuk are two young fellows with no money and nowhere to go. Wait them out and they'll come on their hands and knees to us.

With that in mind, Walter and I set off once again for the Pro Sports office. Our feeling now was that they could contact some hockey people in Sweden and work out a deal for us to play in Europe for at least the 1970–71 season. "Why should we hang around New York and let Francis think he's got us trapped when we can make a good move?" I told Walter. "After all, Carl Brewer left the NHL and had a wonderful time playing hockey in Finland."

Francis had frequently harped on the fact that he determined a player's worth by a combination of his contribution to the team and his appeal at the gate. But Walter and I now decided that the most important consideration was really seniority. In other words, if I accepted The Cat's contract, I'd be the lowest-paid defenseman on the Rangers even though I'd made the First All-Star Team. Francis was dead wrong! So we told Pro Sports what we wanted and then went home to watch *our* club on television.

That was quite a sensation. Walter and I sat there and literally cheered for St. Louis. We wanted New York to lose so Francis would feel a need for us. But we also knew that if the Rangers blew the game it would mean the loss of two points which we'd have to help them make up later, if we came back.

Watching the game, we could see the club missed us. Don Luce and Syl Apps played at center, but neither had Walter's ability. St. Louis won 3–1. After the game Francis was interviewed on television. He wouldn't admit that he'd like to have Walter or me back on the team. He said he had adequate replacements as well as total authority to handle negotiations. And, he reiterated, he didn't need us.

On Sunday Syl came to visit and asked whether the Rangers looked as bad on TV as they had to him. We had to agree. Then we met Marty and Steve, who gave us the moral support we needed. "You guys are right, you're right," they kept saying. But Francis didn't contact us, and the club had a practice scheduled Monday for their opener at Madison Square Garden on Wednesday.

Shortly after the team workout on Monday, Walter and I received a visit from our teammate, Arnie Brown. He had come as an emissary from Emile. Brownie told us straight out that Emile had gathered Bob Nevin, Jean Ratelle and himself to discuss our holdout situation. According to Brownie, Francis wasn't going to budge.

Brownie then said, "You know The Cat means it when he says he won't budge. If you're relying on [Bill] Jennings or [Irving] Felt of the Garden to overrule him, you're mistaken. Emile would rather quit than allow them to do that." I knew Brownie was right, for Emile is a very proud man. Indeed, he wouldn't hesitate to quit.

At six that evening we phoned The Cat saying we'd like to talk with him, and an appointment was made for later that night. Soon after we arrived at his house in Long Beach, Long Island, Emile put on the television set and we all watched the game between Green Bay and San Diego. It was hard to believe the three of us had been battling for so long, because everything seemed just fine. In fact, I almost slipped out of my chair when Emile said, "Brad, how about a beer?" Naturally, I declined on the grounds of my dedication to sport.

Finally we started talking, and it was a true heart-to-heart encounter. Emile explained his situation in detail and readily admitted that he needed Walter and me; and we in turn confessed that we really wanted to play for him. It was by far the best talk we'd ever had.

At last, he said he thought we each deserved $32,500. We said, "Emile, we're only $5,000 apart. Maybe we can account for this next year." He said he'd be willing to consider that, and we said good-night.

Driving home Walter and I figured we'd have to accept his $32,500 basic salary and hope to do better next year when, supposedly, he would make up the $5,000 difference. It was then I suddenly felt a warm surge of confidence in

Francis, a confidence much bigger than the problems we'd been having. This is one guy I'd trust with my life, I thought. Everybody has to have a little faith in something or someone, and for me it was a little faith in The Cat.

Walter and I agreed to practice with the team on Tuesday and meet Emile that afternoon to settle the issue. Let's hope we're on the ice Wednesday night against Buffalo. All of a sudden I'm beginning to feel like a big kid who wants to play. Believe me, it was a brutal disappointment sitting home when the guys left for St. Louis. And when they came back, there I was like a small puppy, tongue out and tail wagging.

I said good-night to Walter and then went home to tell Gerry how things had gone. Wow, what a change! Two days ago I didn't want to talk to The Cat. Now I'm nuts about him. I must be getting fickle.

We worked out with the club Tuesday, as we'd promised, and it was hell. Getting back into shape after four days on the shelf is like climbing the Empire State Building from the basement to the 102d floor. Walter lost nine pounds and I lost six. Then we drove to the city, met with Francis and settled everything.

III

The Season Opens

The day of our opening game in New York—Wednesday, October 14—at Madison Square Garden, so Walter and I had a light skate. I felt terrible. My legs were concrete columns and my body was like spaghetti, the result of an on-again off-again training period.

After the workout I went to the Penn-Garden Hotel, across the street from the Garden, where the team stays on the day of a game. When I got to my room I couldn't fall asleep. I was just too nervous worrying about the game, my return, the fans and all of these together.

Whether it was a coincidence or not I don't know, but my roommate was Walter. At 5:30 we both dressed and went downstairs for some refreshment. He had a cup of tea and I had a Coke. I always like Coke after a pre-game nap; I have a big, thick, sticky taste in my mouth and the Coke clears that away. Walter was as nervous as I was, so we went over to the Garden. I fixed my sticks, taping them and then retaping them, making sure everything was exactly right.

Ed Giacomin walked in. "You'll get a shutout tonight," I told him. Eddie just laughed.

It wasn't a particularly tough game. Buffalo is one of two new expansion teams—the other being Vancouver—and they were playing without their venerable veterans Phil Goyette and Don Marshall, who held out for a while. Neither Walter nor I made a point, but at least I made the scoresheet; I got one penalty for tripping and another for boarding. In the boarding call I really clotheslined the guy with my arm. His body went one way and his head just stayed put. But the penalties didn't hurt us. The fans cheered Walter and me, and we took Buffalo 3–0.

"Walter," I said as we skated off the ice, "let's ask The Cat for a bonus now 'cause we got these guys out of the cellar."

I was happy with myself. The weight was down to 195, and I figured that in a week I'd be in good shape. Only one thing bothered me during the game: I was a bit lacka-daisical, or maybe I should say a little slow in thinking with the puck on my stick. I needed more ice time to get the mental and physical gears meshing again.

The next day a workout was scheduled at Skateland Rink in New Hyde Park, Long Island, where we hold most of our practices. Just prior to that session an interest-ing thing happened, which sheds a revealing light on the sometimes delicate relations between sportswriters and ath-letes, as well as their coaches and general managers.

This particular incident involved Gerry Eskenazi, a pleasant fellow who has been covering hockey for *The*

New York Times for the past six years. It had been Es-kenazi's habit to visit Skateland to gab with us on the days we held workouts there, and most of the fellows had grown to like him.

Frequently Gerry would visit the dressing room before we went on the ice. Usually, however, he'd be alone when he talked to us, so that's why we were surprised this par-ticular morning when Eskenazi was escorted into the room by The Cat. Francis asked for silence, then pulled out a Xerox copy of a page from Eskenazi's book, *A Year on Ice*. As we sat and listened, he read aloud this excerpt about our training camp at Kitchener in September 1969:

"Doors constantly open and shut on Saturday night. Players move down the long hall in waves for ice and mixers, including a ginger ale named American Dry. A prostitute walks the halls, soliciting business from a group of salesmen at a convention. A few younger girls, some per-haps 17, and a few older women in their thirties, also wander around nonchalantly, as though they were headed straight for their rooms. None are guests at the motel though. They have—or hope to have—rendezvous with the Rangers.

"A girl in her twenties comes out of one of the player's rooms, screaming, then sobbing, her hands clutching the front of her unzipped black dress against her neck. She has her shoes tucked under her arm."

Emile then ripped into Gerry, telling him that he'd thrown in that passage just to spice up the book. "How

can you have the face to write such bullshit?" Emile
shouted at Eskenazi.

We felt The Cat was right, because inevitably many of
the players' wives would read it and say to themselves,
"Well, what are these guys doing?"

Personally, I think it's all right for a reporter to write
about what goes on in the games, and to discuss playing
styles and all; but I don't think a newspaperman has the
right to get personal and start writing crap like that.
Eskenazi could get a lot of innocent people in trouble.
To my mind, a reporter should find more elevating things
to report on.

Before throwing Eskenazi out of the dressing room,
Emile told him that he'd been allowed in the room just
about any time he wanted. From now on, he said, he would
only be allowed in after a game, and that was it! Francis
sticks up for his players and takes personally anything
negative written about them. As a player, I can't ask for
anything more.

Emile, as those who play for him know, has a strong
psychological bent. And some felt he had an ulterior mo-
tive in embarrassing Eskenazi in front of the entire team.
The theory was that the contract disputes and the holdouts
had upset our momentum and spirit, and that something
now had to be done to knit us together. Here was a book
all the players objected to, so Francis, by reading it aloud,
had marshaled all the sentiment to his side and had everybody thinking again as a unit, although it was accom-
plished in a most unusual manner.

We then had to face a weekend against the Canadian teams; first Toronto at Maple Leaf Gardens on Saturday night, and then Montreal back home on Sunday. Playing in Toronto is a special kick for me because it's my home town. At Maple Leaf Gardens, as in other rinks, they ask a writer or a broadcaster to select the three stars of each game a few minutes after it's over. One of my childhood ambitions was always to be selected one of the stars and to skate around the ice as they do after their name is called and sort of showboat.

The game started out as a close one, with Gilles Villemure in the nets. This was new, for in past years Francis used Eddie Giacomin in more than 60 games of the schedule, and many thought Eddie was tired by playoff time. However, now it appears Villemure is going to play nearly half the games, so Eddie will be well-rested for the playoffs. After the first period we were down 2–1, but we came back strong in the second to take a 4–2 lead. I got the fourth goal. As I was backing up out of the Leaf zone, I noticed that Toronto center Norm Ullman was going to pass the puck up to center ice. I quickly cut in, intercepted the pass and wound up for a slap shot that beat goalie Jacques Plante high on his stick side.

The final score was 6–2. Rod Gilbert had two goals, and old Walter had two and an assist as well. The team looked sharp. The Maple Leafs, however, are a team of rookies and just couldn't match an experienced club like ours. They were outclassed.

The Canadiens would be another story. They had

finished out of the playoffs the previous year, and that amounted to a provincial disgrace in Quebec. Many people had them figured to bounce back strong this season even though their tough left wing Johnny Ferguson was retired and Ralph Backstrom hadn't yet signed. Before the game Francis gave us a pep talk. He called it a "four-point game," meaning that the Canadiens were a team we'd be battling for a playoff berth. Winning meant gaining two points while the other guys in effect lost two.

The Canadiens are a skating team with some of the fastest men in hockey, and the only way to slow them down is to hit them with your body. Henri Richard, Yvan Cournoyer and Jacques Lemaire, who are small and can fly, shy away from the opposition if they're popped. We call the Canadiens "Frogs" or "Pepsis," affectionate names for French-Candians. All of it's in good humor, as we have several Frogs or Pepsis on our team, including Gilbert, Ratelle and Villemure. It's no secret around the NHL that French-Canadian players—with some significant exceptions —have more style than English-Canadians, but prefer to avoid body contact. And we decided to play to that weakness.

Montreal came out flying and throwing their weight around like Joe Fraziers. Guy Lapointe, Marc Tardif and Pierre Bouchard seemed to be all over the ice using their bodies. But we didn't back up an inch, and so managed a tight, scoreless first period.

In the second period I had my first major fight of the season. And the events leading up to it typify what ignites most hockey fights. In this instance the enemy was Marc Tardif.

Tardif—a strong young forward, six feet tall and 180 pounds—and I collided in a corner, which is normal enough. Still, when this happens the sticks and elbows and thick leather gloves come up instinctively. Now one of three things can happen: the players back off and forget the whole thing, which happens most of the time; the players each wait for the other to back off, finally being peaceably separated by a linesman; or the clash escalates from elbows in the ribs to gloves in the face to fisticuffs. Very simply, it's a case of action and reaction. I got a shot in the nose and decided to retaliate. War was on.

My hands slipped from my gloves a split second before Tardif's, which enabled me to land the all-important first punch. I caught him with a couple of good left hooks before he could do anything about it. Tardif was clever, though, and did the best thing a man can do on the defensive: He moved in fast to smother my arms, and finally managed to lock my right arm under his left. Now it was his right arm against my left. I tried to hoist his sweater to temporarily blind him, but then the linesmen intervened to separate us.

Breaking up a fight is pretty delicate stuff, as the linesmen must carefully extract the proper parts from the mass to make sure one player doesn't get the advantage over the other. This time they made a complete mess of the job, tromping on me so it looked as if I had lost the fight. Of

Next I learned to skate.

Ron and I at peace for the moment.

Everyone enjoyed my ad lib.

A formal family occasion.

The young rocket on the lower left is me.

Robert L. Cornes

Donald Young

One of my first team trophies. March 1961.

Above: This was the check which did for my kidneys as a Junior. I'm wearing 2.

Right: A Toronto Marlboro; and we'd won the Memorial Cup. Can the NHL be far away?

Toronto Telegram

Graphic Artists

UPI

As Dave Balon stickhandles behind the net, I pin one of my favorite foes—
Boston's Derek Sanderson.

The object of my disaffection is Ron Ellis of Toronto.

UPI

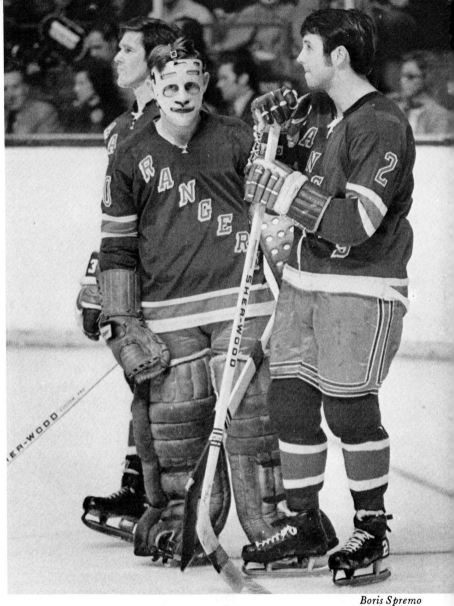

My friend Tim Horton and goalie Gilles Villemure share a thoughtful moment with me.

Above: One of the worst nights of my life. February 19, 1970. My right ankle has just been broken in an accidental collision with Carl Brewer (5) at Olympia Stadium in Detroit. *Below:* Always trouble, Bobby Hull tries to pass me while Dave Balon rounds out the Conga line.

One of the NHL's best stickhandlers, Stan Mikita goes to his backhand to elude me.

Left: My victim is "Super-Pest" Bryan Watson of the Penguins. And if you think my high-stick is illegal, you should have caught his action a moment before.

Right: Sometimes I feel that referees should neither be seen nor heard; and that's how I felt about Bruce Hood (right). Fortunately, lineman Pat Shetler held me stationary.

Barton Silverman

Now I know how General Custer felt at Little Big Horn.

Barton Silverman

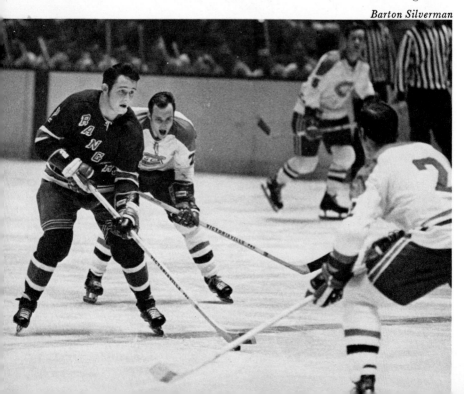

Barton Silverman

Below: Ed Giacomin has just made the save; and now I'm working to keep the puck away from Chicago's Stan Mikita.

Barton Silverman

I seem to be defying the Law of Gravity and Jacques Lemaire of the Canadiens at the same time.

Ken Hodge of the Bruins can sometimes be an awful nuisance.

Barton Silverman

Henri Richard is one of the more elusive forwards in the league; but one day I managed upon him.

"Get that puck out of the zone!"

Barton Silverman

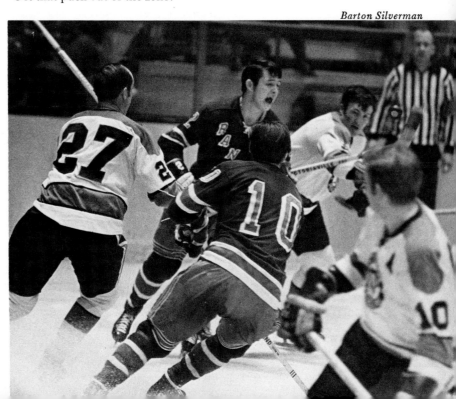

Both photos by Barton Silverman

Above: When an irresist-
ible force meets an im-
movable object (Bill
MacMillan of Toronto),
bodies sprawl.

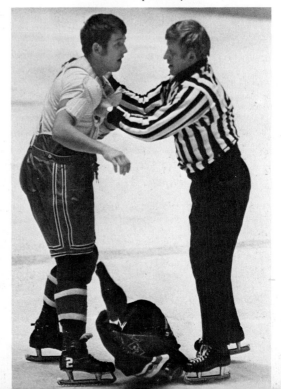

Linesman Pat Shetler re-
strains me once again.

Up, up, and away on Bill
MacMillan's back while
Garry Monahan (20) of
Toronto goes after the puck.

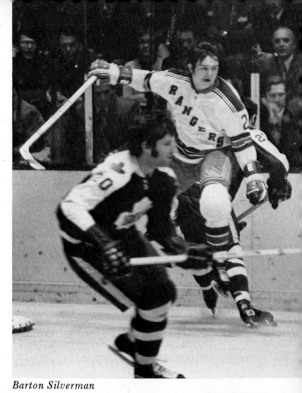

Barton Silverman

Below: I'm not Phil
Esposito's biggest fan, as
Espo (7) is discovering
here. Ted Irvine (27) and
Don Marcotte (29) act as
seconds.

Dan Baliotti

The Cat in a characteristic pose.

Dan Baliotti

Below: Winning! That's the name of the game.

Barton Silverman

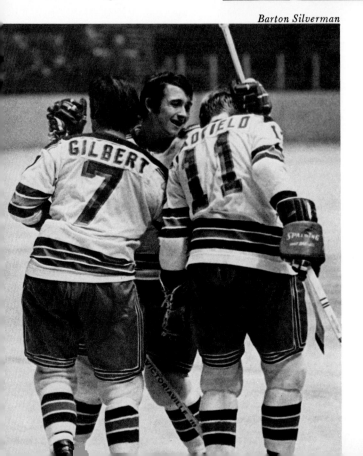

course we both got five-minute major penalties. Nobody was really hurt. The usual case.

When games are tight, like this one, each team plays close to the vest and waits for the other club to make a mistake. There's truth to the axiom, "Hockey is a game of mistakes," and I certainly didn't want to pull a goof that would cost us the game. I didn't. And at 3:26 of the last period, good old Walter stole the puck and put it in, and we won 1–0.

We play nearly 100 games a season, including exhibition matches and playoffs, so it's not easy to get excited every night you're on the ice. But this game featured old-style defensive hockey, evenly matched teams, strong desire on both sides and solid body contact. In short, it was a memorable night.

In mid-October there was a rumor that we would make a deal with Toronto for Norm Ullman, one of the Maple Leafs' top centers. Ullman would be an asset to the Rangers, no question, but personally I was hoping against the trade because we have three good centers in Walter, Jean and Syl, and I like them all. Our defense appears set for the season. There are six of us: Arnie Brown, Jim Neilson, Tim Horton, Larry Brown, Rod Seiling and me. Emile told Larry he's staying, so Larry and Syl decided to find a bachelor's apartment together in Long Beach, where most of the players live. That leaves Mike Robitaille and Jim Krulicki as the expendable players. I'll bet Emile tries to deal them for a draft choice or some future consideration. It's the only logical move because we're loaded with talent both here and at Omaha in the Central League.

Nothing came of the Ullman deal; and a good thing, too. Late October and we're really rolling. We beat Toronto 3–2 at the Garden. I played a part in this one, setting up the all-important first goal. The Maple Leafs had a penalty and I went out on the power play as I usually do. I got the puck behind our net, where we most often launch our plays. Hockey critics believe our game lacks the pattern plays of football, but they're wrong. There are plays in hockey; the difference is that in football you expect them because there's a stoppage and then a play from center. In our game the plays develop during the action, and the beginning and end of each play is not so clearly defined.

When I went behind the net I made a motion with my hand. Center Jean Ratelle caught the signal, and knowing I wanted him to move along the boards, he broke free from his Toronto checkers. He skated over the Leafs' blue line with Hadfield on the left. When a Toronto player tried to intercept him, Jean fed a backhand pass to Vic, who scored.

After the game I reflected briefly on my credits and debits since signing. On the plus side: no goals scored against New York while I was out on the ice in a regular season game. That's the most important criteria of a defenseman's worth. In that department all was well. I'd also been sharp and alert; no complaints there, either. But in the debit area, I hadn't been very effective offensively. I had to shoot the puck more and work harder.

My weight still isn't right. "I can't get the pounds off,"

I told Emile. "I'm still around 200 pounds and I wear a sweat jacket in practice, but the weight just won't come down."

"You're skating well but you're tiring faster," he said, and left it at that. Emile certainly got the message. And now it was extra sprints after every practice.

The Cat is a fascinating man. After a workout he'll bring the team together to examine the mistakes we've made, but he'll never mention a specific player's name. Naturally, though, everybody knows exactly who's being discussed and makes no bones about it, either. After one scrimmage he said, "This one team had a 3–2 lead and instead of protecting the lead in the right way the defenseman who was supposed to be in front of the net wasn't there!"

Two by two, all eyes in the dressing room turned toward Arnie Brown, and Arnie dropped his head and began shaking it slowly.

"One of our forwards," The Cat went on, "is not turning fast enough coming out of the corners." Again, all eyes found Dave Balon, and he turned all shades of red.

There's a lot of play between teammates both on and off the ice. In the Toronto game, for instance, Ted Irvine, our big left wing, received a two-minute penalty for elbowing. As Irvine entered the penalty box I skated over to ask, "Teddy, did you hit that guy with your elbow?"

"Hell, no," he shot back. "I hit him with my fist!"

"Teddy," I said, "you're a bad, bad boy."

Ted, however, was dead serious about the whole thing. He was concerned because after coming to New York in a deal with Los Angeles in the middle of the 1969–70 season, he managed only three assists in 17 games. So admittedly he was worried about staying with the club this year. He'd been given very little ice time and it was getting to him.

"What's the difference between sitting on the bench and sitting in the penalty box?" he asked me.

"Well, Teddy," I said, "when you're in the penalty box you get to skate back."

Our next game, at Minnesota, Irvine wasn't even on the bench, and everybody took notice of that. Eddie Giacomin, one of the better needlers on the club, got on Ted right away. "Now listen," he said, "I want to hear you in the stands tonight. I want you to yell and scream for your favorite team. And I don't care if there are 14,000 people in the building rooting against you. Teddy, go out to your seat and cheer." Irvine had no choice. He did and we won and everybody was happy except Arnie Brown.

Brownie had himself a bad game and he knew it. Like myself, Brownie always feels lousy if he plays a poor game, win or lose. But there was a little more involved this time. Late last season he injured his knee and missed part of our playoff with Boston. Some of the Bruins needled him about "chickening out" of the series. Arnie's knee, however, was so bad that it required an operation during the summer, and now it's not responding the way he hoped it would. His skating is slower and he isn't scoring at his 15-goal pace of the previous year, an all-time record for Ranger defensemen.

He needs a few days off to rest the knee, but he's fearful

that if he takes the days off he'll gain weight, which would be an added problem. Thus Arnie is fighting himself and, I'll bet, thinking, "Maybe I've lost the touch."

Confidence is the secret word in hockey, a word repeated over and over again by players until the word itself has become a cliché. Yet, except for natural ability, it remains the single most important factor in a player's success. Once my confidence goes I know there's only one way to restore it and that's to work harder and harder in practice until I get myself back in the groove. But Arnie's problem is more complicated than that because the harder he works, the more he aggravates his knee condition. I don't envy the fellow.

Still, we're not in a jam because The Cat is using six defensemen. I worked with Larry Brown, a good young defensive-type player, not flashy but who has a surprisingly long reach with his stick, which is a tremendous asset in a defenseman when it comes to poking the puck away from opponents.

Much as I sympathize with Arnie I can't spend my life worrying about him; after all, "Operation Park" is just getting underway and, at last, some results are showing. In the Minnesota game I helped set up two goals and, more important, I was controlling the puck better than I had all month. My skating is improving. Nobody scored on me while our club was at full strength. And my head was right. So right, in fact, that I couldn't help looking ahead to the next week's games, especially the one in Boston on Saturday night, October 31. According to my formula we could put Vancouver, Buffalo, Detroit and Toronto way down below New York, leaving us to battle it out with Montreal and Boston for the top.

The old ego was hanging in there pretty strong—First All-Star, no goals against—until an incident in the dressing room after a game in Bloomington, Minnesota. I was sitting on the bench, sipping a Coke, when a fellow walked in, looked around and sauntered over my way. He stared at me for a second and then asked, "Could you tell me where I can find Brad Park?" And here I thought everybody in the world knew who I was.

Okay, so I survived. But what annoys me is that a reporter—he was from UPI—could sit through a 60-minute game watching us and then walk into the dressing room and not recognize the person he wanted to talk to. Which brings me to the endless "cold war" between hockey players and the press. And, make no mistake, it *does* exist.

Hockey players, as a rule, are skeptical of newspapermen. This is partly the reporters' fault and partly the players'. The players contend that most hockey writers really don't know much about the game: they haven't played it, they don't bother studying it and they don't see what's going on out on the ice. It's not uncommon for a player to read an account and then ask a newsman, "What game were *you* watching last night?"

Reporters need an angle, and sometimes looking for one they blow a story out of all proportion. Seizing on some small incident, they will pump you with questions until they have a story of sorts, but one which is more often the result of their exhaustive probing and fertile imagination than any real worthiness in the subject at hand.

My own pet peeve against some newsmen is that they come to the games looking so careless that when they enter the dressing room, they immediately turn me off. Then their stupid questions lead me to think, "How can I respect this man?" And I'll string him along, because if he isn't sufficiently interested in the game to prepare himself, I'm not going to teach him elementary hockey. I mean, if a reporter asks a fellow who's just scored three goals, "How does it feel to get a hat trick?" what does he expect the player to say? *

Such questions are tossed at us game after game until we've become immunized. Some newspapermen say I have a sense of humor. Well, I hope I do, and I hope I can keep it, because I need it to protect myself from some of the damndest questions. Like Linus needs his blanket.

But, to be fair, there's also the newsman's side. A reporter has a job to do. I recognize that. He's out to get the facts—viewpoints and reactions as well as whatever other insights are available. Unfortunately, many players answer perfectly good questions with the empty reply, "That's hard to say." Which leaves a reporter with nothing. The reason for this is not that most hocky players are stupid, but coming from small Canadian towns are bashful and embarrassed to express themselves, which is really their problem. So because of the skepticism of the players and the inquisitiveness of the reporters, a hostile air exists.

* The answer: "I feel great."

One example was the trouble between Francis and Gerry Eskenazi, after which it was clear that many of the players were going to talk to Gerry with caution, or not talk to him at all.

IV

Boston's Big, Bad Bruins

A hockey team's primary concern is not with the press. Rather, we have to catch and pass our foremost enemies, the so-called "Big Bad Bruins" of Boston. The rivalry between the Rangers and Bruins goes back a long way, long before I was born. Prior to World War II it was the Bruins, led by tough Eddie Shore, going against the Rangers, who had such stars as Frank Boucher, Ching Johnson and the Cook brothers, Bill and Bun.

Later, when Boucher became coach, the competition was just as intense; this time New York sent such skaters as Lynn Patrick, Phil Watson and Bryan Hextall against Boston's "Kraut line" of Milt Schmidt, Woody Dumart and Bobby Bauer. To this day the rivalry has remained fierce, and it's no secret the latter-day Bruins outhit and often outskate the Rangers.

The first major confrontation of 1970–71 took place on Saturday night, October 31, at Boston Garden. Prior to the contest I'd expected a classic because we were a tight, defense-oriented club while the Bruins were averaging five goals a game and hellbent for all kinds of scoring records.

Late that afternoon Mark Mulvoy of *Sports Illustrated* approached me. "What kind of game are you looking for tonight?" he asked. I told him I thought it would be low-scoring. No sooner had I started for the rink than I got the shock of the month; Francis, I learned, had just traded Larry Brown to Detroit for center Peter Stemkowski. This really shook me, as I'd been playing with Brown in the past few games and liked everything about him.

When I walked into the dressing room my heart sank. Larry Brown was hunched over his bench, packing his skates for the trip to Detroit. What do you do, what do you say to a friend in a situation like that? I know he liked New York, that he was settled in Long Beach and enjoyed his Ranger teammates. And now he'd be going against us. It was tough to say good-bye.

"Look, Larry," I said, trying to say something. "When I get to Detroit you give me your tickets, and when you come to New York, you can have mine." It didn't help much.

My prediction of a low-scoring game was half-correct. We scored no goals. But not so the Bruins. They scored six. It was humiliating, both the result and the way it happened, goal by goal. The worst for me, naturally, were those scored while I was on the ice.

We were behind 3–0 in the third period when they scored one against me. I was teamed with Rod Seiling, and right at the face-off Johnny McKenzie of the Bruins got a pass and blew by Seiling. A bit later *we* had the man advantage, and the puck bounced over my stick to Derek Sanderson. He put it on Ed Westfall's stick, and Boston had another goal. It was a mess; nobody was going and we acted utterly defeated. Horseshit.

The loss was bad enough, but the really annoying moments happened a half-hour after the game when we boarded the team bus for the trip to Logan Airport. Most of the players were sitting in the rear and it was quiet. And I mean quiet. I felt so awful I wanted to climb up on the baggage rack and just hide from the world. We'd been humiliated and the bus was like a morgue—until the newspapermen arrived.

One by one they piled in: Dana Mozley of the *Daily News,* Bob Gockley of the *Long Island Press,* Gerry Eskenazi of the *Times.* They were laughing and joking as if we'd won the Stanley Cup. This really pissed us off. Here these guys are supposed to be on our side, supposed to suffer the blows with us. So we're humbled by the Bruins and they're having a ball.

To take my mind off them I began thinking of the previous few hours and about the Bruins and the phenomenon of playing hockey in Boston. And that's precisely what it is. A phenomenon. To begin with, Boston Garden is a zoo; the fans are maniacal and the rink is downright grubby. Without question it is the worst rink in the NHL. It's old and shabby, and always looks as if it could use another coat of paint and at least two more vacuum cleanings. The ice, which goes a long way to determine the quality of a game, is always terrible, and the rink measures 191' long by 83' wide, clearly shorter than the 200' by 85' prescribed in the NHL rules.

All the fans want are blood and guts. And they throw things. Once I was nearly hit on the head by a 45-rpm phonograph record that came sailing down from the upper balcony. And the Boston players are always running at you. This combination gives a visiting player the feeling he's a performer in the Roman Coliseum.

The Bruins have two different styles of play: At home they're bloodthirsty animals, but on the road they're just a good strong hockey team. The "Big Bad Bruins" image is one that has been cultivated in Boston by management. The front office long ago made it clear they wanted a big, hitting team. Players who joined the Bruins underwent dramatic psychological changes. Take Ken Hodge. When he played for Chicago he was a relatively peaceful skater whose primary aim was scoring. But as a Bruin he suddenly started picking fights all over the place.

Another was Wayne Carleton, a teammate of mine in Junior hockey on the Toronto Marlboros. When Carleton moved up to the Maple Leafs he never hit anybody, never fought anybody and was perfectly placid. Then he was traded to Boston and got caught up in the Bruins' syndrome. Overnight he was looking to fight anybody, all the time. Mind you, this attitude prevails mostly at home. On the road there's more lamb in the Bruins, except for Derek Sanderson.

What bothers me most about Sanderson is his flakiness;

at any given time on the ice he doesn't know what he's going to do and he has no concept of hockey ethics. Once when he'd been tripped and was sliding toward the boards, I put my gloves out to keep him from crashing headlong against the wood. So what does Sanderson do when he gets up? Thank me? Never. Instead, he shoves his stick between my skates and dumps me flat on my face.

Sanderson talks a lot about his fighting ability and his willingness to mix. The facts are a bit different. When he does fight, he throws two or three punches and then backs off because he's gotten his shots in and knows he can't handle most guys after that.

Possibly even worse than Sanderson is his teammate Johnny McKenzie. His bag is running at people *from behind*. No player really objects to getting hit straight on, but when a guy rams you from behind that's bad news. McKenzie symbolizes the "bush" style of the Boston hockey club, and it's one that will eventually catch up with them.

Other teams are beginning to look for bigger players, and as these clubs get more beef they'll be able to match muscle with Boston. Montreal is going for such players, and we may too, as in Peter Stemkowski who we already have.

Boston is like the schoolyard bully: Push the little guy around as long as the little guy won't fight back. But when the little guy fights back, the bully doesn't know what to do. That happens to the Bruins. You must play their game. Lay the wood on *them* and get *them* thinking about getting hurt.

Boston did think about this when their defenseman Teddy Green was injured in a stick fight in September 1969 with Wayne Maki, and wound up in the hospital with a fractured skull.

Many people believe Green got exactly what he deserved because he was nothing more than a hatchet man and there's no two ways about it. After he recovered and returned to the NHL this season, I thought he might have learned something from his experience. But he hasn't. He's still carrying that stick high and doing the same dumb things he did before he was hurt.

My point is that there's a major difference between hard-hitting, clean defensemen like Bobby Baun of Toronto or our own Jim Neilson and such men as Green. One episode illustrates my point. We had the puck in Boston's end of the rink. Vic Hadfield took a shot at the goal, and the puck went past Green's head. Right away, Green got the idea Hadfield had shot at him. So what does Green do? As Vic skated away, he swung his stick with both hands and cracked Hadfield across the small of the back, sending Vic down for the count. That's what I mean by a hatchet man —one who'll swing his stick at anybody.

Naturally, I thought Green might have mellowed after the injury, but in our first exhibition with Boston he showed me he hadn't. He was taking runs at guys, laying them out with his stick and upsetting me because when you see a guy swinging the lumber that way you say to yourself, "Jesus, the next time he may get me between the eyes."

Right from the start I steeled myself in Boston. I matched every Bruin player blow for blow. Each time one hit me I'd give it right back, until they developed a respect for me. Match the Bruins blow for blow and they change completely. They start contemplating: "These guys are also tough. They're fighting us, matching us." Francis realized this and that's why he's brought in big men like Stemkowski and Irvine instead of such fancy types as Phil Goyette and Don Marshall. The Bruins have turned present-day hockey into a brutal sport, so the other clubs need some size even if the big guys lack talent. Of course, size alone won't win hockey games; we must also match Boston's talent.

The basic difference between the two teams, apart from their hitting style, is the existence of Bobby Orr in the Boston lineup. He gets the puck out of their zone and shows the other Bruin defensemen what to do with it. He draws the enemy center toward him, and he draws the opposition winger, then he makes a safe pass to his other defenseman who's by now had time to skate free.

Another thing about Orr is that he doesn't like to get hit, and sometimes he'll throw a cheap shot at one of our guys. A man of his ability needn't revert to such stuff, but he does. Naturally, it makes us a little wary of him, which is probably his intention. The trick is to hit Orr cleanly and get him good and angry. The problem, however, is to catch him.

V

Staying in Contention

After Saturday night's debacle in Boston we didn't come back to our New York City base, the Penn-Garden Hotel, which we usually do when there's a game Sunday. Instead we returned directly to our homes in Long Beach. The plane ride was as quiet as the bus ride; nothing was said, and that goes for Francis, too. If we had won, he'd have come around to say, "Way to go, fellas." But a loss, or even a tie, isn't good enough for him, and the next day he'd explain what we'd done wrong.

I think he's a good coach. He treats everybody on the club as an equal and he doesn't let anybody get away with anything. There's no question about his absolute authority in running the club. Some people may question his policies, but I don't because they've worked well so far.

Still, he's a hard guy to understand. If he had his way each one of us would get about the same salary on the theory that nobody would then have occasion to beef. I have to respect Emile, because after our contracts were signed he never bugged me about what I was getting. Not once did he say, "Brad, you weren't worth your salary tonight." That's not his style. His philosophy is simple: "Hockey is a business. If we win, we make money. You make money, I make money; everybody makes money. As long as you put out for the club you'll stay here, and you'll be making money." But not as much as I'd like to make.

The difference between Francis' coaching and at least one other style became evident to me early. In my rookie season Bernie Geoffrion was our coach. "The Boomer" went with the older players and kept young guys like Walter Tkaczuk and myself on the bench, even though we'd had good camps. So the team dropped to sixth place, Geoffrion got sick and Francis replaced him.

Unlike Geoffrion, Francis goes strictly by ability. He took a chance with Walter and me, and the club snapped out of its losing streak and finished third. I learned that Francis is not afraid to take a chance, which impressed me as much as the fact that he likes to give his players responsibilities. He wasn't afraid to use a rookie like me to kill penalties. I said to myself, "This man is giving me a chance to prove myself, so I will!" And I did. And when you make a mistake he'll let you go out on the next turn to redeem yourself.

Francis didn't panic after we were beaten 6–0 by Boston. Our next skate was Sunday night, November 1, at home against the Black Hawks. Before the game The Cat ripped us, but only as much as we deserved. Then we went out and whipped Chicago 5–2 in a strange game.

The unusual part was that Bobby Hull, a very calm and gentlemanly player, blew his stack late in the game. It happened when Hull tried to break into our zone and was intercepted by Syl Apps, Jr. Syl sort of tackled Bobby from the side, and the two went down in a heap. As they climbed to their skates, Bobby smacked Syl across the face with his hockey stick, and then proceeded to use Syl as a punching bag.

We have a club rule that if any one of our guys is getting beaten up in a fight someone rescues him. In this case Vic Hadfield was the first man over the boards, and he pulled Hull off Syl. Except for a few cuts here and there, Syl escaped undamaged. The real damage came later in the week when Stemkowski replaced him on the third line with Bob Nevin and Ted Irvine. Syl was dropped to the fourth line with Jack Egers and Ron Stewart, a unit that hasn't been getting much ice.

Of course, the mere presence of Stewart on the Ranger club is something considering the problems he had in the summer of 1970 when Terry Sawchuk got hurt and eventually died in the hospital. I'd been out of town when a friend of mine called to say that Sawchuk was in the hospital, but we had no idea how serious it was until later.

Then I asked my friend what had happened and he told me there had been trouble between Stewie and Ukey, which was Sawchuk's nickname. The two of them were roommates in a rented apartment near Long Beach and they had different life-styles. Stewie is the type of guy who'd be impossible to live with because he's so prim and proper.

With him, everything has to be just perfect. For example, when he goes on the road he takes his own pants presser. And he's an immaculate dresser with immaculate taste in everything. This perfectionist style would get on Ukie's nerves, and he'd say, "That Goddamned Stewie, he's always immaculate."

One night after the season, Stewie and Ukie went out for a few drinks. Stewie said something to Ukie about the phone bill or the rent, and Ukie just said that he'd had enough of Stewie and started going after him in the bar where they were drinking.

That was broken up, but then when they got back to their apartment they started in again on the lawn. Ukey fell over the barbecue and got badly hurt. He died a few days later.

After that there seemed almost a code among the players that nobody was to say a thing about any of this to Stewie. We were going to carry on normally, just as though it was the previous season and nothing had happened, except we were without one of our teammates. As if Ukie had been traded away. By the same token, there hasn't been any needling of Stewie by the opposition. It's understood in a situation like this that needling is out of bounds.

Stewie is the club's elder statesman and one of its humorists, although most of his gags carry "X" ratings.

The opposite of Stewie is Jean Ratelle, who is the most serious, dedicated player on the team. Ratty enjoys the fellows but, basically, he has three interests in life—his family, hockey and the stock market, with maybe a little golf on the side. That's it. Period. It doesn't matter whether we're in Oakland or Pittsburgh or Montreal, the first thing Ratty does is buy a newspaper and check the stock quotations. He's absolutely obsessed with finance.

Arnie Brown is another serious guy I liked to needle, knowing Francis was getting more and more upset with Arnie's rushes into the enemy's defensive zone. "Geez, Arnie," I'd tell him, "you weren't forechecking enough last night. You've got to forecheck better." Actually, of course, he should be back on the defensive line with me. But at times I'm not there either.

Once I nearly had a fit after carrying the puck over center ice toward the opposition's end. I figured Arnie was back covering up for me when I heard this guy yelling for the puck as I moved to the blue line. I looked to my left and there was Arnie; we had left the forwards behind on defense, and Francis was yelling and screaming, so I gave Arnie the puck and dropped back.

Most of the time our kidding is harmless, but once in my rookie year Walter Tkaczuk, Reggie Fleming and Stewie were playing on the same line. Stewie and Reggie were veterans who believed a first-year man could do nothing right. They'd give Walter the business no matter what he did. We'd be sitting in the dressing room between periods and Reggie would natter in Walter's left ear and Stewie would natter in his right ear. Between the two of them, Walter was going nuts.

One night Walter got up off the bench, took two steps forward, turned, looked them both straight in the face and said, "Stewie. Reggie. Bug off! You guys stick with me and I'll show you how to play this game."

From then on everything was fine.

When you have 18 men on a team inevitably there is friction. Bench-warmers resent the fact they're not playing regular. One goalie wants to play more. The practices are too often, too long, too hard. The possibilities are endless. But sometimes, just when you think there will be trouble, nothing happens.

One example is the mixture of Syl and Stemkowski. When Stemmer arrived he bumped Syl off a regular job. On top of that, Stemmer arrived preferring Detroit to New York and not wishing to play for the Rangers. So Stemmer and Syl, both fighting for the last center ice job, wound up as roommates. Knowing Syl as I do, I know he'd never bad-mouth Stemmer. Also, the club is winning with him, and there's no arguing with that. So Syl is just sitting back, waiting for his chance. This is an agonizing situation, which I went through when Geoffrion was coach. Sitting on the bench, hoping somebody will break a leg so you can play—it's the most natural reaction in the world.

A similar situation exists between our goaltenders, Eddie Giacomin and Gilles Villemure. Giacomin has always been our number-one goalie, and such back-up men as Don Simmons and then Sawchuk played very little. That was fine with Eddie because the more work he gets, the better he feels.

But in the last four playoff years New York has been

eliminated in the first round, and Eddie was fingered as being responsible for the defeats because he was tired and, consequently, not as sharp as he should have been. It's a difficult charge to substantiate. Eddie, who would know best, insists he *wasn't* tired and, except for a game here and there, was as sharp as ever.

Whatever the case, this year Francis decided to make a major change. He brought up Villemure, an excellent minor-league goalie, and is using Gilles as much as Eddie. So far the plan has worked pretty well and we're right up there battling for first place. But I know Eddie isn't keen about it because, as he's said, he needs as much regular game work as possible.

On Tuesday, November 3, we held a practice at Skateland prior to flying out to Oakland for our first West Coast swing. We were worried about Billy Fairbairn, the right wing on Walter's line. As a rookie last year, Billy had a strong year and was expected to do even better this season, but he's been looking sluggish and seems tired all the time. My own guess is that he's got mononucleosis. If true, it could finish him for the season.

The next night we went up against the California Golden Seals in Alameda County Coliseum, a beautiful rink across the bay from San Francisco. Traveling from New York to California for a hockey game isn't easy for two reasons: the change from chilly weather to balmy dulls your enthuisiasm for hockey, and the time difference upsets your metabolism. Both showed in the awful way we played. The Seals, a poor team, beat us 3–1; and we didn't score our goal until the third period.

After the game the defense crew got together for an impromptu conference over a few beers. Tim Horton, Jim Neilson, Arnie Brown, Rod Seiling and myself. We agreed that our problem was the manner in which we were coming out of our defensive zone with the puck. Arnie and I felt it would be best to have a forward in the corner, ready for a pass. If he's covered, the pass will go instead to the defenseman in front of the net, assuming he's uncovered. We know Francis doesn't like this play, but we're convinced it's the safest way to clear the puck away from an onrushing line, especially Boston's where the offense comes at you in a wave. Our plan provides three escape valves— a winger, the center and the other defenseman—and should make it a lot easier to move the puck up ice.

By contrast, Francis' plan is to have one defenseman act as a shield for the other, who is behind the net, and to skate in front of their center to cause some interference. But since that leaves only a split second in which to make a pass, it's more difficult. Having the extra valve seems better, and so we'll see what happens. We all expected a brutal practice the next day after losing to the Seals.

Emile fooled us. The workout wasn't half-bad, although he had every right to be furious. "Sometimes," he said, "you're going to lose games, but you have to give the other guy credit when he deserves to win. The Seals deserved to win last night."

Afterwards a group of us planned "the Shave," an initiation ritual we give to every rookie. Although it's a bit primitive, it's become a tradition on several NHL teams and we're one of them. What we do is shave the guy—who is held firmly by his teammates—from neck to toe. And I mean from neck to toe. We don't omit a hair. While painful and on the cruel side, Syl went through it, although not very happily. Francis came along in the middle, took one look and walked away laughing. He really likes this kind of thing; considers it a manifestation of team spirit. Who knows, maybe he's right!

Syl has been terribly unhappy, and not only because of "the Shave." Later on, he and I went out for a few beers and he told me his problems. "I'm getting fed up with the scene here," he said. "I'm not getting ice and I'm ready to quit."

Syl went to Princeton University but never got his degree. He left college to play professional hockey, and I knew that going back to graduate was on his mind now. "Don't be a horse's ass," I told him right off. "You want to be an NHL player, and you'll be a good one."

"Do you want to know why you're not playing more?" I asked. "For several reasons. You're a hell of a good skater, but you're going full speed all the time instead of alternating your tempo and waiting to get the puck before making a break. You're going so fast you get in your own way. Another thing, you're not shooting the puck right; it's a flip shot and there's no power behind it. You've got to work on your shot."

After I left Syl I wondered whether my diatribe would

have any effect on him. When I saw him the next day I found out. He wouldn't talk to me, ignored me altogether. "Geez," I said to myself, "maybe I shouldn't have said anything to the guy."

Then, a day later, he came over to me and we talked as if nothing had ever happened. That's the way it is sometimes. It took Syl two days to digest what I'd said and to realize I wasn't attacking him but only trying to be helpful.

Our next game was to be on November 7 in Los Angeles. Before we hopped the plane from Oakland, we found out that Billy Fairbairn does have mononucleosis and will have to return to New York for a long, long rest. Right now the guess is that he'll miss about four weeks.

One man's suffering is another man's joy. Now Jack Egers, who was a star in the 1970 playoffs against Boston, will get a chance on Walter's line against the Kings. Maybe he'll regain his old form.

To prepare for a game, I like to do some private reconnaisance work on the enemy. This was possible against the Kings because they held a workout the day of our game with them, and I sat in the stands and studied each player.

Los Angeles is a big club but weak offensively. And the defensemen will never win the Norris Trophy. Only three are of any consequence—Larry "Hank" Cahan, who played for the Rangers ages ago; Matt Ravlich; and Gilles Marotte. Considering each has been dropped by several NHL clubs, it's difficult to worry about the Kings' defense. To beat Los Angeles all we need do is put pressure on their defense early in the game. Score a few goals and laugh all the way to our win.

It's a sin to come to the West Coast for two games and not leave with at least two points; that is, if your club has designs on first place, which we do. Besides, St. Louis walked into Boston Garden the other night and actually beat the Bruins 2–0 in Boston!

Prior to the Los Angeles game I lay on my bed thinking about the Kings, and I gradually built them up in my mind to be a pretty good hockey club. "For God's sake, Brad," I told myself, "they've got a lot of players who've been around the NHL for a long time. They're going to be big trouble tonight."

Slowly my opinion of the Kings changed from one of contempt to one of great admiration. I had actually psyched myself out for the game. Luckily, I caught myself in time.

"Look, man," I said, "these guys are nothing more than expansion players. Larry Mickey, Paul Curtis, who am I kidding? If they were any good they'd be with established clubs. But, instead, they're players nobody else wants. So a few have played in the NHL for a while, still we should whip them!"

The Kings came out with a rush, checking well and sending two men in on our defense to try for the puck all the time. It's a fact that on any given night the worst team can jell and the best team can falter. Eventually, however, class asserts itself.

This time it took about a period and a half. With the

score 3–2 in our favor Tkaczuk and Egers were both battling King defensemen for the puck in the Los Angeles end of the rink. Meanwhile, I'd just climbed over the boards on a defensive line change. I skated like hell for the blue line, and got there just as Jack threw a pass back. I slapped the puck into the upper left corner of the net. That made it 4–2 and put us out of danger. We cruised in for a 6–2 victory.

We departed Los Angeles tied with Montreal for first place, the Bruins one point behind. Not bad, Rangers.

The bosses of the NHL don't like to admit it, but there is a considerable difference between the expansion teams and the established clubs. With a few exceptions, the new teams lack big stars and high scorers. So they must rely more on intensive team play and basics, especially close-checking, which means slow hockey.

Of course, I can't blame them. The prime concern of any team is to win games, and fans in expansion cities want their teams to win no matter how. Pittsburgh really doesn't care whether its team wins a tight-checking boring game, as long as they win. In New York, Boston and Montreal, however, fans like wide-open play.

On Wednesday night at the Garden, Pittsburgh gave us an excellent demonstration of how frustrating an expansion team can be. In all honesty, the Penguins are not an exciting team. Coach Red Kelly is a terriffic hockey mind but he's not playing anymore. Their offense is weak, and their defense isn't much better. I like both their goal-

80   PLAY THE MAN

tenders, Les Binkley and Al Smith, but they're not enough to sustain the team. Yet, somehow, the Penguins made the playoffs last year and somehow they've managed to win or tie games this year, and the way they do it is very interesting. They employ a form of hockey hypnosis. The Penguins mesmerize you, and while you're still in a daze, they score a goal or two and come out with either a win or a tie.

We should have buried Pittsburgh the way we were playing in the first two periods, building up a 3–1 lead and completely outclassing them. Then those Svengalis in the blue and white uniforms came on in the third period and lulled us to sleep. They do it by not antagonizing the opposition. They don't check hard and they give the impression the game is over, causing you to surrender your vigilance—and the puck. Once we lost our concentration, they burst through and scored twice. Result: a 3–3 tie, which should have been a victory for us.

This time Francis wasn't gentle. He got us together the next day and cracked our asses in practice. Emile also gave me an ultimatum—lose five pounds in ten days, or else!

"You're a split second behind the play," Francis said. "That split second is vital because it's throwing all your moves off and you're reacting poorly. We need your offensive power, but because of your weight your passes aren't sharp. Now, get with it!"

I told him I would, and as I walked out I looked at the calendar. Friday, November 13!

I had no choice but to go on a crash diet, which was tougher than you might imagine. A night later in Chicago the guys went out for a few beers before dinner. I just sat there and stared. Ugh! The only thing that saved me was the repartee. Somebody brought up the name of Forbsie Kennedy, and the stories began to fly.

One was about how the club kept Forbsie from breaking curfew and drinking too much beer. It seems they roomed him with the chief scout one night when the curfew was 11 P.M. Sure enough, Forbsie was in the room at 10:45 with the scout, when he turned to him and said, "Listen, can I go down to the candy store and get a chocolate bar to tide me over until morning?"

The scout said, "Sure, go ahead." Forbsie took off, and nobody knows to this day whether he got his chocolate bar or not. But this much is known: He didn't get back to his room until 5:30 the next morning.

Our bull sessions can often be cheering. I once asked Tim Horton, who's been in the league almost as many years as I've been alive, "Don't you get fed up with pro hockey after a while?"

"To me the game is still fun," he said. "But most important are the fellows on the team. If you enjoy them— and I do—then the game comes easy."

That made sense, and since I like my teammates I enjoy hockey at the moment. Which is not to say I'm fond of every character on our club. But this is where self-hypnosis comes in. To be successful it's necessary to *believe* in every person on the team. One can't be best friends with everybody. But the moment we step on the rink, everybody wearing a Ranger sweater is my buddy. You must over-

look the blemishes because the name of the game is team-
work.

That's why I'm pleased Francis had a heart-to-heart talk
with Syl. Lots of rumors were circulating about trades,
and that Syl would be involved in one. But Emile left Syl
with a real sense of confidence in his game. He wanted to
give the kid some encouragement. And if Syl can play
more and get experience, he should become a big asset to
the club.

As for myself, on the 14th we played the Black Hawks in
Chicago and I really loused things up. Perhaps I should
add that I had the help of referee Bob Sloan.

It happened this way. Sloan had given me a penalty early
in the game which I know I didn't deserve. We killed it
off and everything seemed all right. We were ahead 1–0
in the second period when Chicago got two successive
penalties. That gave us a 5–3 advantage in skaters, and we
figured to wrap up the game right then.

We had the Black Hawks bottled in their own end when
Stan Mikita, their veteran center, managed to tip the puck
past me at the blue line. Tkaczuk cut across to intercept
him, but Mikita faked Walter and cut in toward our goal
for a shot at Gilles Villemure. Meanwhile, I had pursued
Mikita to where I was within reach of him with my stick.
As he started his shot, I shoved my stick under his, lifted
it off the ice and forced him to miss. A perfect play. I was
congratulating myself when, all of a sudden, I heard a
whistle. I turned and there was Sloan motioning me off the
ice for hooking. I couldn't believe him, but when the

thought registered that, yes, the penalty was for real, I let Sloan have it with every profanity in my vocabulary.

"That was one of the most horseshit calls I've ever seen in my life," I shouted at him. "And do you know why? Because it was cheap and you called it to even things up, and that's one of the most ignorant things a referee can do."

Just as I feared, Chicago scored before I returned, and went on to win the game 2–1. Right then, all I wanted to do was forget Sloan, because if I kept thinking about him I'd have shot the puck at his head. On the other hand, when I cooled off a bit, no doubt I felt responsible for the loss, so I tried to pass the blame off on an official. I was awfully upset.

We flew to New York for a Sunday night game against Toronto, and I roomed with Walter. Before leaving for the rink the two of us watched the world championship stock car race on television, and an interesting play developed. The fellow who'd been leading by several laps got knocked off at the last minute by the runner-up, who made a great last-minute swerve to win the race. There are times when you plan so perfectly and then—boom—everything is fouled up.

That night we beat Toronto 4–2, but we didn't expect to gain on the first-place Bruins because they were playing the Golden Seals, a very weak team, in Boston. At 11 P.M., though, the score came over the radio: California 2, Boston 1. We were tied for first again.

Another turnabout was the reaction of New York fans

to our right wing, Bob Nevin. As far as hockey players are concerned, Nevvy is a very solid, two-way player who does his job efficiently and without fanfare. A strong skater with easy movements, Bob may give the impression he really isn't trying. Which is not the case.

New York fans, who have some understandable gaps in their training because so few of them have ever played hockey, don't appreciate Nevin's qualities, and they've been on him constantly. Of late, Nevvy has really been shaken by the fans, but against the Leafs he got back at them by scoring a beautiful goal and setting up Teddy Irvine for the clincher. By the final buzzer our fickle followers were chanting: "WE WANT NEVIN, WE WANT NEVIN!"

The club was due back in Los Angeles for a game on Wednesday, November 18, but I got there two days earlier to do a television show with football players Merlin Olsen and Roman Gabriel, as well as baseball player Brooks Robinson and actor Peter Lawford.

When I arrived in L.A. I took a cab to the Hollywood Roosevelt Hotel, cleaned up and then went for a walk along Hollywood Boulevard. The thought occurred to me that here I am, all of 22 years old, and just a couple of years ago I wouldn't have dreamed I'd be where I am today.

Hollywood dazzled me. I walked past Grauman's Chinese Theater and took in all the sights—especially the girls. The fascinating aspect was the difference in attitude compared with New Yorkers. The kids seemed to be a lot looser in California, whereas in New York everybody seems to be colder and more uptight, and more bizarre.

I sat down in a hamburger joint on the boulevard and stared at two women in their sixties. They were painted from head to toe. Their fingernails were bright red; their lipstick was bright red. They looked like they had been sitting in that spot for 60 years waiting to be discovered.

Two days later I paid the price of my early visit to Hollywood. I met the team at the airport and was called Rock Hudson, and asked the whereabouts of my leading lady.

Then Walter started getting on me about my weight. What he does is hold off until Francis is in the vicinity. For instance, at the airport he shouted very loud and clear, "Hey, Brad, how's your weight?"

Anybody within ten feet could hear what he said and, naturally, Francis was only about five feet away. Whenever Walter does this to me, Francis responds by giving me a lecture, and Walter just turns away laughing.

Out in L.A. once again, we put the Kings through a little bit of hell Wednesday night. They ran up a 3–1 lead midway in the second period. Then I stole the puck from Ross Lonsberry inside the Los Angeles zone, fed Jean Ratelle and he shot it under Denis DeJordy's pads to make it 3–2. We got a fluke goal to tie things at 3–3, then walked away with a 5–3 win.

That made the flight to Montreal somewhat more tolerable—because the flight conditions were terrible, the trip lasted seven hours and there was no movie. So what else to do but have a few drinks, which several of the fellows did. One friend of mine appeared to have a drink too many, and when it came time for practice the next morning, he didn't show up. Francis was furious and called a meeting for 10 P.M. that night. "If you're on this team," he said, "you have to expect to take it on the chin if you do something wrong."

A $500 fine accompanies the first major warning. If there's a second time you just get your ass out of New York, which is another way of saying Francis will trade you to another club. But I don't think he's actually done this since I've been with the team.

I'd guess that Francis reprimanded my friend for not setting an example. He is a veteran, and Francis expects him to show the proper attitude. Later I took him aside and asked, "What happened?" He smiled, no doubt recalling the night before. "Well," he said, "that's one way to cure your fear of flying."

We were in Montreal for the traditional Saturday night game at the Forum. Playing the Canadiens in Montreal is always something special, because every player knows that hockey is kind in the Province of Quebec and a fierce pride seems to ooze out of every crack in the old building.

One great night! I was able to unload two of the best bodychecks of my career, first against John Ferguson and then against Jean Beliveau. They were hip checks, delivered by throwing my hip out at the last possible second and hoping the opponent flies over my back. These checks were made famous by the late Bill Barilko, who played de-

fense for Toronto in the late 1940s and early 1950s, and
who was a good friend of my parents. Barilko scored the
winning Stanley Cup goal in the 1951 playoffs, and then
he was lost in a flight over the Canadian northland. My
dad always wanted me to be a player like Barilko.

The Ferguson check was one defensemen dream about.
He had just gathered the puck at his blue line and begun
cutting to center at full speed when I set off on collision
course with him. By my own estimate, there was no way
I could miss him.

But Ferguson is the type of player who likes to run right
over you. So when I came within a few feet of him, I pre-
tended to go high on him, and quickly Ferguson leaped at
me. The second he jumped, I thrust out my hip and sent
him ten feet in the air. He landed on his head and shoulder. Fortunately, it wasn't his nose, because if that nose
of his gets any bigger, he'll have a difficult time finding
the rink. Of course, this would indeed be a good thing for
us, because Ferguson is the guts of that Montreal hockey
club.

In the third period Beliveau, who can do a few tricks
with the puck, nearly skated past me. Once again, I shoved
my hip out and just managed to get a piece of the big guy.
He went down—and so did the Canadiens, 5–4.

I'd like to cash in those bodychecks for a reprieve from
Francis on the weight ultimatum. By Sunday night, November 22, I was to be down to 195, and it was touch and
go. At breakfast Walter made it tough for me. I limited

myself to grapefruit and tea, while he countered with home-fried potatoes, eggs, toast, the works.

"Y'know, Brad," he said, "I watch my weight. If there's one thing I do it's watch the food I eat." Then he paused and kind of drawled out the rest: "Yeah, I watch it go from my plate to my mouth."

Just to get an idea how I was doing, I got on the scales that afternnon. I held my breath as the indicator settled. I was 195½ only half a pound overweight. I immediately put on the heavy rubber sweat jacket, laced on my skates and spent some time on the Garden ice. Back in the dressing room I was down to 194, and dipped to 192 after the game that night, a 2–0 win over Minnesota.

Gilles Villemure was in the net, and he single-handedly saved the team. This can happen in hockey. A club can be flat as flat on any given night, but still come out on top if it gets first-rate goaltending and capitalizes on a mistake or two of the enemy's. "How does it feel to be a second-stringer?" we kidded Giacomin after it was over. But the fact is, the way Gilles has been playing, Gilles is the team's number-one goalie. For the moment at least.

A sad incident during the game muted our celebration. Jack Egers, in the middle of a rush down the right wing, was about to cross the Minnesota blue line when he appeared to be knocked slightly off-balance as he shot the puck. A split second later Jack was really creamed by Fred Barrett, the tough rookie defenseman. Jack toppled over, hitting his head on the ice with a tremendous wallop.

Instinctively, we all knew Jack was in trouble. Big

trouble. Our trainer, Frank Paice, skidded out on the ice. When he reached Jack he realized the gravity of the situation: Jack had swallowed his tongue and was within minutes of choking to death. Paice had a pair of tongs, forced Jack's mouth open and finally got his tongue out of his throat.

But, unfortunately, that wasn't all. Jack had suffered a severe concussion, and he left the ice for further examination. When we went to the dressing room between periods, Jack was sitting on a bench.

"Jack," I asked, "how are you?"

He looked straight ahead. I don't think he even heard me. He was in a total daze, and was finally removed from the dressing room in a wheelchair.

All of a sudden we're beset by one woe after another. Vic Hadfield is out with a groin injury, Jack Egers is gone for God knows how long, and on Wednesday my defense buddy, Arnie Brown, was rushed to the hospital for a kidney examination.

The next night we were in Philadelphia when who walks into the dressing room but Brownie. The hospital X rays had proved negative, so he'd come to Philly to play. Not the sort of thing a baseball or basketball player does.

Of course the motivation was there, for Francis had brought up Ab DeMarco from Omaha in the Central League. Jim Krulicki and Don Blackburn were up front as replacements. These new guys give me a creepy feeling because on the one hand you have to accept them but on the other they're after our jobs.

I've got to be careful because if I go bad Francis will give DeMarco a chance. The coach's barometer is production and production alone. Sorry to say, the production against Philadelphia was one goal for us and three for them. I wound up in a big fight with a left winger on the Flyers (I still don't know his name). His number was 18, and I'd taken him into the boards all quite legally when he whacked me in the neck with the stick.

I took a dim view of this and punched him between the eyes, the only thing to do under the circumstances. Well, he didn't appreciate my punch any more than I'd enjoyed his crosscheck, so he retaliated. I lost my balance, and the next thing I knew he was on top of me. Somehow, I regained the edge and clambered out from under. Except by then we both were exhausted and the fight was over. But if he ever tries another crosscheck like that, I'll get him.

My philosophy on hitting is simple enough—when I hit an opponent I'm going to hit him clean and he should expect to be hit. But if he brings his stick up or gives me a cheap shot, then I'll play just as dirty and will give him shot for shot.

Whether I know his name or not, I'm going to give him a chunk of my body every time he comes down my side. This is to test him. If his stick comes up he'll be in for some bad times. Of course, I expect to get clouted every so often because hitting is part of the game, and you either learn to live with it or you find another job.

Occasionally I get the feeling I'd like to do something else. Such a thought came to me on Thanksgiving Day.

This is a great time for turkey or roast beef or ham and to say thanks to the Lord—if you're not a professional hockey player. But instead of being home, I was in Buffalo for a game with the Sabres.

What made it worse is that the Sabres have no right being in the same league as the Rangers. They're no better than a good minor-league club, and yet they came out of it with a 2–2 tie. Expansion clubs just have a way of dragging the better teams down to their level. We're not playing good hockey; we're out of the groove. And we have a Saturday afternoon game coming up in New York against the Bruins of all people.

A few may think it strange, but after the Buffalo game I went out for drinks with my parents, my aunt and uncle from Toronto and none other than Reggie Fleming, who now plays for the Sabres. An hour earlier Reggie and I were trading head feints; now we were bantering across the table.

Needless to say, I wouldn't do this with 99 percent of our opponents, but Reggie is something special. When I was a rookie he was one of the few Ranger veterans who gave a damn about me and really helped me out. People have labeled him a hothead. True, perhaps. Except whenever Reggie blows his stack it's for the benefit of the team. He's a strong and very loyal team man.

On this particular night Reggie was heckled at the restaurant. As so often happens, a guy came over to the table and said, "Fleming, you're nothing but a dirty hockey player." Reggie smiled in return. "Maybe I am rough," he said, "but I'm afraid I haven't the finesse of Jean Beliveau or Bobby Orr."

There is a very human aspect of hockey. Reggie is a friend, even though he is my foe. Likewise, in certain game situations, opportunities arise to really cream an opponent, but I ease up a bit if he's a friend. A perfect example occurred in the Buffalo game when Don Marshall, a former Ranger, skated down my side.

Now, I could have rocked his cavities with a bodycheck if I'd really wanted to. But I didn't because it's simply not in me to destroy a friend just because he's wearing a different color jersey. The same holds for Phil Goyette, another classy guy who once played for us but now skates for Buffalo. Of course, if either of them happens to make me look bad or scores on me, then I might just belt him after all.

The same philanthropy I share for Phil and Donnie cannot be bestowed on the Boston Bruins, who we play Saturday. There's not a man on the team I like, and there are several I dislike very much indeed. This time we're at home, and I've got a few scores to settle after the 6–0 whipping they gave us up there.

The game was a lemon. We just caught the Bruins, 3–3, in the final minutes of play when I set up Bobby Nevin for a goal. But we were stale again; so stale, in fact, that Boston scored twice while we had the man advantage. And if that doesn't shake you up, nothing will.

For me, though, the game had a little extra meaning. I got into a fight with Wayne Cashman, who is one of their toughest. Naturally they started the trouble. Cashman's linemate, Phil Esposito, took a run at Dave Balon in the corner. Nothing more happened until play moved to the other end, and this time Esposito ran at Bill Fairbairn.

About Esposito. He's an extraordinary stickhandler and a superb shooter, but he doesn't have any guts. He's carried in that department by the animals on the Boston team. Esposito runs at people from behind. After he ran at Fairbairn, I moved in because I expected more trouble. And I was right.

When Cashman hit me with a high stick, I didn't waste any time. The gloves were off in a jiffy and I popped him three good shots in the face before he could do a thing. A minute later, as we skated to the penalty box, Cashman snapped, "I'm going to get you."

"Look," I laughed, "if you keep your stick down I won't have to hurt you."

Don't get me wrong. I don't pride myself on my fighting. Perhaps Sanderson and John Ferguson do; but I've got some hockey ability. As for Cashman, it was a simple flare-up. I won't hold a grudge against him, unless I get the worst of it. Usually, of course, no real damage is done in a fight. Physical damage, that is. At times, however, one player intimidates another. The Bruins like to do this, although when one of us faces up to one of them, he's never quite as tough again.

Canadians and Americans differ about hockey fighting. The Canadian is inclined to deplore it because he knows how the game should be played. He's been brought up with it. Fighting is *not* hockey. The game is stickhandling, passing, shooting, clean bodychecks and goaltending. That's what it's all about.

American fans are something else. Many of them cry for blood the minute the puck is dropped, and the night isn't complete without at least one full-scale brawl.

Real hockey is somewhere in between. Nobody can deny that fighting is part of the game. Fans appreciate it, and for players it relieves the tension. Yet I don't consider fighting a major aspect of my game; it's bodychecking and puck-carrying and, if I'm lucky, an occasional goal.

Sunday night, November 29, I got a chance to show that I'd regained my All-Star form. We were at home against the sleep-inducing Penguins and I was nearing the top of my game. Only one item troubled me, my sticks. I made a deal this season with the Sher-Wood people to use their hockey sticks, but I was having trouble finding just the right size and turn of blade for me. Right now I have a moderate curve in the stick blade; something between one-quarter and three-eighths of an inch. I prefer a light stick, weighing about 19 or 20 ounces, but with a stiff shaft.

The longer curve on my stick allows me to control my passes better, both forehand and back. I like the light, stiff shaft because it enables me to feel the puck on my blade. This is important because a player is supposed to skate with the puck, his head up and looking for the opposition as well as teammates. By getting good "radar" from stick to puck, it's easier to carry the puck without looking down.

When I shoot I don't like the stick to be whippy. I want it to feel solid, like a baseball bat cracking against a ball.

The bat doesn't bend, and I don't believe a stick should either. My shot is considered hard, not quick. Rod Gilbert, for example, has a quick shot. If both of us shot the puck at a piece of tin, my shot would dent the tin more but his would get there first. I was hoping to put my shot to good use against the Penguins.

Pittsburgh threatened to follow the old put-New-York-to-sleep pattern. We took a 4–0 lead in the second period and were laughing when, all of a sudden, Pittsburgh got one goal and then another. Now we had only a two-goal lead with the whole third period to go.

Eddie Giacomin was feeling awful in the dressing room between periods. He'd seemed half-asleep on the first goal, and he knew it. As often happens when we're in trouble, Eddie tried to shake us up a bit. "Look, you guys," he called out to the defensemen, "don't let them shoot. *Not at all!* Don't let them shoot, Brad! Don't let them shoot, Arnie! Don't let them shoot, Chief! Don't let them shoot, Sod! If they don't shoot they can't score, and if they don't score we'll win."

The warning buzzer sounded. There was a shout and we were up, tromping down the rubber matting leading from the Garden dressing room to the aisle and then out to the bright lights, the organ music and the cheers. It was another sellout crowd of 17,250, and they were impatient with us after blowing two goals. Perhaps I could do something about it right away.

On my first shift I found the puck loose behind our net. I grabbed it and saw Andy Bathgate, the Penguins' veteran, move quickly toward me in an attempt to snare the puck. As Bathgate lunged, I lateraled the puck to my right —pretending to give it to him, then taking it away. Since there was plenty of space ahead of me directly up the center, I took off in that direction with Jean Ratelle. I looked from side to side and realized that both Ranger wingers were covered, so I continued with the puck until I reached the Pittsburgh blue line, where Penguin defenseman Dunc McCallum came at me.

I swerved left, and when he went with me I tried desperately to cut back right. He managed to partially block the puck, but not quite enough to take it away, and it wound up on my right skate. In one motion I booted the puck back on my stick, took a stride past McCallum—who by now was caught flatfooted—and discovered the only man between me and the net was goalie Al Smith.

My only impression was of a one-foot opening between his pads and the right goalpost. "Put it along the ice," I told myself. "He's liable to catch a lifter." The shot stayed low and Smith moved late. It was in! A dream come true. After years of listening to Foster Hewitt broadcast, "He shoots, he scores!" on the Canadian network, I finally fulfilled my dream of making an end-to-end rush and then scoring. A picture goal, and it finally happened to me. I was the most surprised guy in the world.

On the next shift, Giacomin gave me a "Way to go, Brad" as I circled the net. "Had to get it," I told him, "because I'm afraid they're going to get a couple of shots on you before the night's up."

That made the score 5–2, and then, to make the night complete, my buddy Syl scored on a backhander for his first NHL goal. I couldn't have been happier. It reminded me of my first NHL goal—against Boston in a 9–0 win. Mine was the last goal of the game and, it turned out, Syl's was also. A 6–2 victory.

VI

All about Me

Slowly but surely our wounded are returning to the
lineup. Jack Egers says he's ready, but he'll need a pro-
tective helmet—the only guy on the team to wear one—and
it will be interesting to see how he responds after that head
crack. Billy Fairbairn is supposed to be over his mononucleosis, so if those two are tip-top we'll be in fine shape
up front.

I'm still having problems with my weight. After losing
four pounds I discovered that I'd put them right back on
a few days later. Another difficulty is that some of the old
warriors took me to a terrific Italian restaurant on the
East Side of Manhattan called El Vagabondo. From the
outside it looks like a real dive, but the food is fantastic
and there's a bocci court right next to the tables. The wine
is also fine, and my waistline's in trouble again!

We're laughing though. We beat St. Louis 4–2 on December 2, and I surprised myself on one play. It was in
the second period when Christian Bordeleau of the Blues

blocked a shot by Jim Neilson and grabbed the rebound. Bordeleau is one of the fastest skaters in the league, and had the jump on me for what looked like a clean break-away. Yet I raced after him, actually caught him from behind and took the puck right off his stick. Frankly, I never thought I could catch the little guy.

That was my smile for the night; the other belonged to Vic Hadfield. We were sitting beside each other on the bench when I saw a banner hanging in the upper reaches of the Garden. It read VIC, I LOVE YOU. When I pointed it out to Vic he laughed and said, "Guess where my wife, Myrna, is sitting tonight?"

The next day we got a bit of bad news. Claude Ruel, the fat little coach of the Montreal Canadiens, has resigned and will be replaced by Al MacNeil. Ruel was a funny little guy, and I feel sad about his leaving.

Claude is a French-Canadian who never really mastered the English language, so he'd always be yelling from the bench with a curious mixture of French and English. The night I played my first All-Star game in 1970, Ruel was our coach. I was sitting next to Gordie Howe when Gordie gave me a poke in the ribs and asked, "What in hell does 'Don't stop to skate' mean?"

"Beats me," I said. Gordie then pointed to Ruel, who was leaning over the boards shouting at one of our guys, "Don't stop to skate." Of course he meant "Don't stop skating." By this time the whole bench was laughing. Montreal will miss him. And so will I.

It's a funny thing how coaches come and go in the NHL.

A year ago Bill Gadsby was fired after winning his first two games. Imagine that, he was batting a thousand and they let him go. I understand there was a lack of communication between Gadsby and Red Wings' owner Bruce Norris. Or, perhaps, too much of it. Gadsby wanted to run the team his way, while Norris had other ideas. Norris had a special telephone hookup from his box to both the dressing room and the bench, and was always on Gadsby's back. If a coach is going to run his team properly, he must have complete authority. And Peter Stemkowski, who was with Detroit at the time, told me that Gadsby was a hell of a good coach. He was fair and square, and he knew the game well. But Norris owned the team, so that was that.

My rookie year we had some trouble too. Boom Boom Geoffrion had taken over as coach that fall at training camp. He'd been a terrific hockey player up to just a short time before my arrival. And I remembered him as one of the NHL's leading scorers. He frightened me at first because I thought he was a real rough guy—mean and tough. It was only later I discovered he was putting on a show, and that he really has a heart of gold. Those first days of camp I was the only player to gain weight; and so The Boomer would keep me after practice and put me through skate sprints until my tongue was hanging out. I was terrified of the man. If he'd told me to go through the end boards, I'd have gone through them.

Early in the season we climbed to first place, but then in January we started losing and tumbled to sixth. Just as it seemed we were snapping our slump, Geoffrion got an attack of ulcers and Francis took over. But I've always felt there must have been something more to it than that.

Whatever the case, Francis took over, gave me my big break and I've been a regular with the team ever since. Francis has complete authority over the team, and he uses it to his advantage. There's no question who's boss. Unlike Norris, Ranger president Bill Jennings leaves Francis alone. Emile has told me that if he doesn't continue to have complete authority he's going to leave New York. And I'm sure he would.

On Saturday night, December 5, we were to play Toronto at Maple Leaf Gardens. Going up against the Leafs on their rink is always a homecoming for me because I learned hockey within a stone's throw of the Gardens.

It all started for real when I was six. My brother Ron, who is two years older, was already playing organized hockey. But when he wasn't involved in a game, he'd play with me on a makeshift rink out on the front lawn. There was a big tree right in the middle of our rink which he would skate around while making his rush.

Even though Ron was older, I could still skate as well as he. But I wasn't old enough for organized hockey. That really upset me, and I used to wail and bug my father to get me into the league. I figured he had pull because he was a referee. He wouldn't give in, although he did take me along to the games.

One day I got my break. The regular goaltender didn't show up so I knew there was a spot for me. "Hey," I told them, "I'm a goaltender. I'll play goal." Actually, I didn't

know much about goaltending, but I thought it was worth
a try. So I put on the skates and the pads and went into the
nets, and the next thing I knew some guy came tearing
down the left wing at me.

I hugged the right post but he shot the puck into the
left corner for a goal. I immediately started to cry. My
mother, who was standing right behind the net, called out,
"What are you crying about, Brad?"

I wiped the tears from my eyes. "That guy's not supposed to shoot it in there! He was supposed to shoot it
here!" But I smartened up, stopped the crying and played
goal for about three games after that. Whenever an opponent came in on a breakaway, I'd just throw myself
across the goalmouth and dare him to score. It was primitive goaltending, I'll admit, but it worked because kids
that age couldn't lift the puck. Overnight I became "Mr.
Zero," the shutout king. Then the regular goaltender returned and reclaimed his position. Since the fellows saw
I was a good skater, they let me stay with the team.

This didn't last long because my brother and I were so
good we'd take the puck and skate and stickhandle right
through the opposition. We wouldn't pass to anybody else.
So the officials finally asked us to leave because we were
hurting the league.

We joined a more competitive league in the Scarbor-
ough section of Toronto. My team was the Eglington
Aces and, at seven, I was named an assistant captain. I
played the "Atom" age division, for boys nine and under.
When I moved up to the "Peewee" division, I met Syl

Apps, Jr. My father was coaching us at the time, and we were so good we got an invitation to play at the International Peewee Hockey Championships held in Quebec City. There was no question we'd reach the finals—which we did—but what happened then was interesting.

Prior to the final game our record was 29 goals scored and only one scored against us. By the middle of that championship game we were ahead 6–0 and really running away with it. After the second period, Dad came into our dressing room, put his foot on a bench and gave us the word: "Okay, fellas, we're by far the best team, but let's not make a shambles of this final. I want you to ease up; pull back on your shots. When you have a good shot on net, miss it. I don't want you to embarrass these guys. I don't want any more goals unless you have no choice."

On the first shift of the last period, Syl won the faceoff and passed the puck back to me. I went to their end and passed it to Syl and then we just passed it back and forth, never letting them touch it. Finally we moved in on their goalie. Bobby Griffin, our leading scorer, had the puck right in front of the crease. Their closest man was 15 feet away, and all Griffin had to do was pop it home. Instead, he passed back to our man at the point. The second that happened the crowd started booing and Dad benched us. Needless to say, we won the championship.

Playing on a team my father coached wasn't easy. Once, we won a game 6–0 and he came into the dressing room and blasted us. "You guys got a shutout," he said, "but you made mistakes left and right."

Next time we won 1–0, and he said we'd played a great game. He was a fickle coach. A few years earlier he'd dropped my brother because he didn't think he was good enough.

Dad emphasized fundamentals. Skate, shoot, check. Those were his favorite words. He insisted I engage in a lot of body contact and learn to take an opponent out of the play. This wasn't easy because I was one of the shortest kids around. I didn't reach five feet until I was 14 years old. I couldn't knock down the big fellows, so I'd fall in front of them.

My father was also strong on puck control. "Never give it away," he'd say. "Make sure you know where it's going before you pass."

I give him credit. He worked hard with me when jobs were hard to find and we didn't have much money. At home we'd drink powdered milk—and I can't stand powdered milk. We'd cut corners every way possible. Finally, however, he got a job with Allstate Insurance when I was 12. Even so, he'd plan his work schedule to mesh with Ron's and my hockey playing. I'd play a game at 6:30 P.M. and my brother would play at 8:30 P.M. When I was through, I'd hang around the rink playing chase with my teammates through the tunnels under the seats.

But the rink had a professional quality as well. The sideboards were enormous. In fact, they were so high we'd never climb over the boards and plop to the ice because the six-foot drop would've killed us. Instead, the coaches would take us around the waist and lower us out of the benches, gently, to the ice.

Throughout the early years my brother and I sustained a keen rivalry, which I'm sure helped me more because I was younger. Ron, who was a bit better, whet my appetite for competition. And I always wanted to beat him at everything. Of course, he'd get mad a lot. And if I was winning, he'd deliberately pick a fight and beat hell out of me. But this simply made our rivalry the more sweet. One night he really leveled me during a game between his older team and mine. Yet back I came. My advantage was our parents. They favored me because I was the youngest. Now, of course, I feel bad about it. But I loved it then.

When I was 15, Dad was transferred to Montreal, so we moved there and my brother and I tried out for the same Junior B team. He was really hurt when I got a spot on the club and he was rejected. For me, the experience was tremendous. My bodychecking was now quite effective, and I was finally growing. In six months, by the time my father was transferred back to Toronto, I'd become all of 5 feet 8 inches tall.

This turn Dad was asked to coach the Neil MacNeil High School Junior B team, an affiliate of the Toronto Marlboros, who were linked directly to the Toronto Maple Leaf organization. Naturally, I was asked to play for Neil MacNeil. I got a hockey scholarship, with all expenses, tuition, books, uniform—everything paid. Besides that, they gave me $2.50 for each game. At 16 I was a professional; I was actually being paid to play hockey. I couldn't believe it.

I played terrific hockey for my father at the start of the season, but then he got into a dispute of some sort and quit. The first thing the next fellow did was bench me, so that was about it for the year.

The next season a funny thing happened. The Neil Mac-Neil team folded and I became a free agent. I then got a super invitation to go to the Hamilton Red Wings Junior A camp. My stickhandling, skating and bodychecking were jelling neatly, and I was all set to leave for the Hamilton camp when, the night before departure, I got a phone call telling me not to report. "The Toronto Marlboros have put you on the priority draft list," a voice told me. Jim Gregory, now manager of the Maple Leafs, was the Marlboros' manager at the time, and he'd pulled the rug right out from under me. Well, I was wild; but I wasn't quite sure what to do about it. My father said he'd talk to Gregory and see what could be done.

Gregory told Dad straight out that he didn't think I was good enough to play Junior A hockey. "Well," my father said, "I think he *is* good enough. And if you don't think so, then why don't you let him go to the Hamilton camp where they do?" This stopped him. Gregory finally agreed to let me come to the Marlboros' A camp.

Well, that was some humiliating experience. I'd just turned 17, was 5-10 and 173 pounds, and I showed up the next night, raring to go. I went up to one of the trainers.

"Excuse me, sir," I said rather timidly, "but I need some equipment."

"Is your name on the list?" he snapped back.

I told him my name and he said it wasn't on the list. Then I went to a second and third trainer until I found the one with my name on his list. He dug into a bag and pulled out some grubby old equipment and told me this was the best he could do. I walked over to the bench where the Junior A guys were sitting. Every one of them had on the spanking new uniform of the Marlboros. They looked like aces. I looked like a vagabond.

What could I do? I dressed and went out on the ice, where I found Jimmy Keon, kid brother of Dave Keon, the Maple Leafs' center, and Jimmy Davidson, son of Bob Davidson, the Leafs' chief scout. They had both played Junior A hockey the previous year and were beautiful skaters. Meanwhile, there I was flopping all over myself.

When the skating workouts began I singled out these two and matched them, stride for stride. At first I was really awkward, but I pushed myself, learning to take the longer, smoother strides they were taking, until I could stay with them.

The camp was divided in half: the out-of-towners, who'd come to Toronto to try out with the Marlboros, and the in-towners, guys like me who lived in the city. I was still smarting from Jim Gregory's insult and determined to make good. On my first shift in the opening scrimmage, I lined up Brent Imlach for a bodycheck. Brent was the son of Punch Imlach, the Maple Leafs' manager-coach, and a pretty good forward at that. As Brent skated toward me I waited, and then—whomp!

A little later a forward named Terry Caffrey—so shifty he could hang jockstraps—came in on me, and I sent him flying as well. That's all my confidence needed. From then on I knew I had a shot at one of the two defense openings.

There were three regulars—Jim McKenny, Brian Glennie and Doug Dunville. I was competing against a big, strong fellow named Jim Casidy and a chap from Calgary, Randy Murray, who would fight anybody. I knew Murray was the type of player the Marlboros preferred, and I also figured the battle for that fifth spot would be between us. Right then I decided it would be a good idea to confront Jim Gregory about my future salary with the Marlboros. That's how cocky I was. So I went to his office and immediately asked him if I was going to make the club.

According to Junior A regulations, the most a player could earn at that time was $60 a week. And when I asked Gregory about making the team, he replied, "That depends."

"Well," I went on, "could we talk money?"

When he heard that he grabbed me by the shoulders and pushed me into the next room and snapped, "Sit down there."

I knew he was playing tough but I couldn't keep from shaking, since I'd never confronted anything like this before. "All right," he said, "let's talk money. What do you want?"

"Jim," I said, "if it's okay with you I'd like $50 a week to play Junior A and $30 a week if I play B."

"You can't have it!" he roared. "I'll give you $40 and $20."

"No," I said, "$45 and $25."

He smacked his hands and said, "You got yourself a deal."

As it turned out, the Marlboros sent Randy Murray to the Junior A team in London, Ontario, and I stayed with the Marlboros A club as the fifth defenseman. I'd made it on my first try.

Then a second funny thing happened. We went on the road to play an exhibition game against the Tulsa Oilers, a Leafs' team in the Central League. The game was played in Kingston, Ontario, and we beat them badly. But I was still on the bench, because I was fifth man, until one of our regulars broke his hand in a fight. I then moved into the regular lineup and my game came together. So when the season opened, I was the number-four defenseman.

Our opening game was against the Oshawa Generals on Maple Leaf Gardens ice. There were 11,000 attending that afternoon because Oshawa was led by none other than Bobby Orr. I'd heard a lot about this blond defenseman, but I had no idea how to play against him. I found out on my very first shift.

Orr got the puck and started on one of his patented rink-length dashes, coming directly at me. Bobby had been in the league three of four years and was a little older, so I watched him carefully as he cut toward center ice. I was getting ready to poke the puck away from him when suddenly I tripped and fell flat on my back. Orr went around me and passed to a teammate who scored. My first shift in my first Junior game.

Somehow I steadied down after that and kept my spot as fourth defenseman throughout the season. We finished fifth out of nine teams that year and had a pretty good club. Our goalie was Al Smith, recently with Pittsburgh. Up front were such skaters as Wayne Carleton, Terry Caffrey and Gerry Meehan. In the playoffs we reached the semi-finals against Kitchener. We had a tie in the final game with 11 seconds remaining when Walt Tkaczuk came down ice for Kitchener. Walter is a left-handed shot, but on this play he switched hands and beat Smith to win the series for Kitchener.

The second year was an even better one for me—until the playoffs. Again we were up against Kitchener; and in the opening game I got into a fight with Don Luce, later my teammate on the Rangers. During the fight Luce raised his head and gave me a beautiful eye.

The next game I was carrying the puck down the ice and I decided to take a shot. When I dropped my head for a split second because I couldn't see the puck out of the swollen eye, one of their defensemen, Sheldon Kannegeisser, hit me a vicious check that tore the ligaments and a cartilage in my right knee. Although this put me out of action for the rest of the playoffs, we beat Kitchener and went on to win the Memorial Cup, Canada's Junior championship.

Unfortunately, this wasn't my only serious injury as a Junior. One night I hit a fellow named Ralph Stewart with a hip check, and he went tumbling heels-over-head in the air. As he flipped over, his knees caught me in the kidneys. I was hospitalized for nearly five weeks.

I didn't start thinking seriously about an NHL career until my third Junior year. By then I'd become Rangers' property, a result of the Junior draft, and Francis approached me about signing a contract.

Emile, visiting Toronto in May 1968, said he'd like to see me. At the time, because I was trying to finish my Grade 13 high-school exams, I sought to postpone our meeting until June. But my father was adamant. So I met with Francis to discuss money.

"Emile," I said, "I'd like a two-year contract."

He offered me $6,000 if I played in the Central League and $12,000 for the NHL, as well as a $3,000 bonus for signing. "That's a pretty good deal," he said.

I didn't think so. "I'm thinking along different lines," I told him. "I'm thinking of a two-year NHL contract for $35,000—$17,500 a season. Or, for the Central League, a two-year contract for $25,000, with $10,000 to sign."

When Francis regained his composure he rejected the proposal. And it was at that point Dad cut in with his, "First, Brad, you have to prove yourself in this league before you make any outsized demands." Then followed the brief back and forth which I covered earlier on.

The contract came a few days later. I signed it, mailed it back and waited impatiently for the $6,500 to arrive.

Though I'd vowed not to buy a thing until I received the check, I did get my parents a swimming pool. When the money came, I was teaching at a summer hockey school. I ran home and put the check in the bank until December. Then I got myself a Dodge Charger.

My next obstacle was the NHL itself. I had the money, but I had to make the team. Training camp was at Kitchener Memorial Gardens, and when I got there I realized the only fellow I knew was Al Osborne, who'd played with me on the Marlboros. He was surprised to find me practicing with the Rangers while he was working out with Omaha. But I'd insisted on being with the Rangers to see if I was good enough, because I'd learned as a kid that the way to improve is to play with people who are better than you.

Nobody knew me at camp, while the rumors had it that if any young defensemen were to crack the lineup they would be Al Hamilton and Mike Robitaille. The Rangers had been eyeing Hamilton for a long time, and Robitaille was the best defenseman on the Kitchener Junior club. But I didn't care. I watched the regulars carefully, saw that I could skate just as fast as they could and shoot harder. So, maybe I wasn't as smart. I'd learn.

"Do what you think you should do," I kept telling myself, "and don't worry. If you've got the puck and there's nobody free, go with it yourself. Make a play."

After the workout I sat in the stands with my parents, who'd come over from Toronto, and talked with a couple of newspapermen. They asked me if I thought I'd make it as the Ranger fifth defenseman.

"No," I told them, "I expect to be fourth." And I meant it.

Each day I developed more and more confidence. I also minded my own business. Once I left the ice I returned to the Holiday Inn where we were quartered and watched television. I didn't even go out for a beer. And by 11 P.M. I was asleep.

Of course, I wanted very much to talk to some of the veterans—Rod Gilbert, Eddie Giacomin and Bob Nevin— who I had seen on television. Except that I was shy. "What can I say to them?" I asked myself. And since I didn't have the answer, I stayed very quiet for most of camp.

One reason was my embarrassment after the first day. I'd met Bob Nevin that summer at the hockey school, and had talked to him quite a bit there. So when I saw him the first day at training camp, I gave him a big "Hiya, Nevvy." He wouldn't say a thing, ignored me completely. And that really hurt. Later on, however, when it looked as though I might make the club, the guys opened up a bit. Giacomin began explaining defensive maneuvers, and veteran Harry Howell offered a few pointers as well.

Sooner or later, every rookie is put to a test by one of the more rugged pros on the team. I got mine from Vic Hadfield. During an early scrimmage I threw a legitimate bodycheck at him, and as I skated away he cuffed me with the back of his glove. I cuffed him back, and he cuffed me again. At the other end of the rink we started the same thing once more. But as I didn't back away an inch, everything was peaceful after that. I'd been accepted.

Off the ice the needling was much tougher. Ron Stewart, who can waste a man with words, really gave me the business when he discovered my parents had visited camp. "Brad," he'd ask, "did your mother bring you cookies and milk? Are they coming to New York with you? Have you bought them a house down there?" The only thing to do in a situation like that is to laugh along with your protagonist. For if I'd been marked as a thin-skinned rookie, I'd really have had hell to pay.

I stuck with the big team right up to our first exhibition game against Montreal in New York. One reason, of course, was that I'd been having a good camp and was neck-and-neck for the fifth spot. And when Robitaille dropped out leaving just Al Hamilton and myself, we became surprisingly good friends fighting for that empty position.

During most of that game against Montreal I skated around doing very little, but later on I stopped a rush just inside our blue line and took off with the puck. I saw Rod Gilbert on my right and only Jacques Laperriere on the Canadiens' defense. Automatically I passed the puck to Gilbert, not wanting any part of it. All of a sudden I noticed the puck being passed back to me. I was 30 feet in front of the net, and just rifled it toward the goal, up and up into the corner of the net. The fans cheered my first goal on New York ice. I was the most surprised guy in the world. Not long after that Francis called me into his office, and I was given a one-way plane ticket to Buffalo.

"We've been promising Hamilton a chance," Francis told me. "He deserves one good shot at it, and we don't want you just sitting on the bench where you won't get any experience. In Buffalo you'll get lots of ice time and you'll improve. If we call anybody up from Buffalo, you'll be the first."

Hell! What did I care about their promise to Hamilton; I was a better defenseman, and I had proved it in training camp. What else is a man supposed to do? Still, I comforted myself, Buffalo wasn't all that bad and I'd be getting the same salary and I'd get plenty of ice. And I did like Buffalo, as things turned out. I shared a house with three other fellows on the team, paying only $25 a month rent, and saved more than I've ever saved in my life.

All in all I played 17 games for Buffalo, had two goals and 12 assists. Pretty solid. I played plenty and my confidence soared. Walt Tkaczuk was also playing right along with me until New York called him when Orland Kurtenbach was hurt. Then, early in December, I got the call; Hamilton was being sent to Buffalo and I was going up.

At first it was like heaven. The club was winning and I was playing really well under coach Boomer Geoffrion. But when we started losing, Boomer benched me. "Jesus Christmas," I said, "I don't like this. I'm not learning a thing on the bench." Then in January Boomer started playing me again. And then he was replaced by Francis.

I never saw the bench again. The season had a terrific ending. We made the playoffs and I even got a few All-Star votes. The only black cloud was our playoff series against Montreal.

I contributed to a costly mistake in the opener at the Forum. The score was 0–0 and we were more than holding our own at the time, when I cleared the puck down ice because we were shorthanded. Larry Jeffrey, one of our penalty-killers, chased after it, thinking the sides were even. When he touched the puck, we were called for an offsides. The face-off was at our end of the rink, Montreal got a goal, and we were sunk. They took the first two games at the Forum and the next two in New York, and that was it.

The summer following my rookie year I was in New York when I got a phone call from Francis. He asked if I'd drop over to the Garden for a chat. I was hoping he'd give me a raise, but when I arrived, he invited me to walk him down to the dressing room. Once there he turned on all the lights. I was befuddled. I couldn't figure out what he was looking for unless it was a new stick. Instead, he motioned me over to the scale and told me to get on. I weighed 204 pounds.

"That's not too good, is it?" said Francis.

"No," I replied sheepishly, "it's not."

"I don't want you coming to camp like that. You'd better be around 196, or else!"

Sure enough, the minute I got to camp in September 1969, Francis pointed to the scale. I weighed 196, right on the button.

The second year was wonderful. I started off like a house afire and the team went well from the start. By mid-season

I had made the Second All-Stars and was invited to play in
St. Louis. The thrill of a lifetime, except I almost didn't
make it. We had just played in Minnesota where the temperature was 26 degrees *below* zero. When I woke up Monday morning I had a temperature of 102 and was feeling
worse by the minute. But I had to grab a plane for St.
Louis, which I did.

Monday night was the All-Star banquet, and I barely
survived it. My temperature remained 102 all Tuesday,
and when I dressed for the game that night I felt like hell.
I alternated with Carl Brewer, Jacques Laperriere and
Bobby Orr. When I teamed with Bobby, we were the
youngest pair ever to play in an NHL All-Star game, and
he was a real godsend. I'd just throw the puck over to him
and say "Go!" By this time I was too sick to do anything.

From time to time my second year, people would bring
up that applesauce about a "sophomore jinx." I simply
laughed. Even Francis got into the act. He wanted to sign
me to another two-year contract for $15,000. "Nothing
doing," I told him. "Twenty-three thousand."

"What happens if you don't have a good year?"

"Don't make me laugh," I said.

The year was a tremendous one, until that February
night in Detroit. We had the Red Wings 2–1 and the puck
was coming along the boards. Frank Mahovlich was playing left wing when I moved up on him to keep the puck
in Detroit's end. My shot hit his stick, bounced in the air
and went by him. As I was chasing toward the corner after
it, I noticed that Brewer was skating at me. I was going too

fast to avoid his bodycheck, so I calculated that the best thing for me to do when we collided was to go *over* him. All of a sudden my right skate caught on something, and the next thing I knew my right skate was behind me, my whole leg was behind me and I was falling.

I fell into Brewer's hip and he collapsed on my ankle. Bam! The pain shot through me like an electric current. I thought I'd broken my shinbone because the agony was so intense, snapped it in two with my whole knee gone and everything.

At the Detroit Orthopedic Hospital they X-rayed the leg. My doctor was a winner. He gave me a six-pack of beer and let me drink while they put the plaster on the broken ankle. By the time they were through I felt wonderful, singing along with them through the final stages. Then who should walk in to see how I was but Carl Brewer, a real sportsman. There are few like him in the NHL.

The doctor said I was through for the season, but I told him I simply couldn't stay out that long. I wanted to be back on the ice when we visited Detroit again, and certainly ready for the playoffs.

For many years the Rangers' team doctor was a popular Japanese-American named Kazuo Yanigasawa. So when I returned from Detroit after the accident, I went to Dr. Yanigasawa's office to have my cast changed. He kidded with me, as he always did, with that big cigar plugged in his mouth—the trademark of Dr. "Yana."

Later that day he died.

Dr. James Nicholas, who followed him, told me that before I could expect normal use of the leg I would have to wait for the bones to fuse. "The only way it will break again," Dr. Nicholas said, "is if you do the very same thing to it."

At first getting mobilized was next to impossible because it was stiff. Eventually, when my cast was removed, I thought I'd just whip my leg right out of there. Instead, the leg was like a dead piece of wood; I had no control over it.

After a few days I went out to Skateland. Just me, owner Al Eisinger and the ice. I took a few turns and gave up. "I've had it," I told Eisinger. "I'm through for the year. There's nothing there. The leg hurts. I can't use it. And I'm actually limping when I skate."

However, the next day there was a 500 percent improvement. I wasn't limping. I could spring off the leg and do so much more that as I kept improving in the succeeding days, I began pestering Francis to let me play.

He finally let me test the leg against Montreal toward the end of the season. Of course I knew there was no way I could rush up the ice with the puck and still have the speed to get back, so I decided to play a defensive game. On my very first shift I hit three guys and felt good again. We came off with a 1–1 tie, then played the Canadiens again the next night and beat them. This time I scored a goal on the power play.

I was able to help the team in their stretch drive for a playoff berth. But then we came up against Boston in the series opener and I hurt myself again. This time we were eliminated in six games, but considering that Jimmy Neilson, Arnie Brown, Rod Seiling and I all had injuries of one kind or another, we handled ourselves pretty well I feel.

Oh, yes. I made the First All-Star Team that spring along with Bobby Orr. This made me think a bit. I recalled how a lot of people had ignored me when I was a kid because of my size; how Jim Gregory of the Maple Leafs tried to do the same when I wanted to play for his Marlboros' A team; how my father persisted in my behalf. And I'm sure the same Jim Gregory could have used me when we skated against his club that Saturday night, December 5, at Maple Leaf Gardens.

From time to time Emile will do some interesting things, such as switching roommates. I'd been rooming with Tkaczuk, but on December 5 Francis roomed me with Syl and put Walter in with Eddie Giacomin, hoping a switch might break Walter's scoring slump. The plan worked— but not for Walter. Eddie beat Toronto 1–0 and Stemkowski got the big goal.

The Canucks are ripping along in the East Division. The main reason is their captain, Orland Kurtenbach, who is not only one of the better players in the league but is also king of the NHL fighters.

Kurt wasn't any trouble Sunday at home. But a young forward, Rosaire Paiement, battled with Hadfield, and Vic made the mistake of punching him on the head. Vic received a broken hand and will be lost four weeks. That's going to hurt our first line unless Jack Egers can fill the bill. We beat Vancouver 4–1 and now must grab a jet out to British Columbia, where we play them again Tuesday night.

Everybody has been closely watching Egers' comeback after his severe head injury suffered on November 22. Jack is now playing with a big helmet—the only guy on the team with one—and he's taking some needling. "Hey, Cannonball," is our standard line because he looks like one of those circus guys who's shot out of a cannon.

After Jack's accident the usual cry went up that helmets should be required in the NHL. "Did I walk off?" Jack asked when reminded of the incident a few days later. "I don't even remember going out on the ice to start my shift." Then he reflected a moment and added: "When something like this happens to a player, he starts thinking about his family. Sure, I'll wear the helmet. I didn't wear one in the past because nobody else on the team wore one and I thought I'd look dumb."

Al Eagleson, advisor to the NHL Players' Association, has been campaigning for the helmet to be made mandatory, but I'm still against it even after what I saw happen to Jack. My last year of Junior hockey I wore a helmet because it was required, and I found it an awful nuisance. I perspired terrifically when I wore it and, in a cold rink, the sweat would freeze between my head and the helmet, giving me a headache. Often the helmet would slip over my eyes, so I couldn't see the puck and didn't know where I was going.

Even worse, I discovered that players on the opposition were taking advantage of me just because I was wearing the headguard. The enemy would bring his stick up more quickly, as he assumed I had extra protection. They'd try to scare me in the corners by tapping me on the helmet with their sticks. Nonhelmeted players had no compunctions about high-sticking the guys wearing them. So we were coming out of games with more and more cuts around the eyes.

But that's only part of the reason I don't think helmets are for me. From the viewpoint of ego and crowd appeal, helmets take a lot away from the game. They tend to make all players look alike in a game where personal identification is important. Since Stan Mikita of the Black Hawks began wearing a helmet he has lost much of his personal appeal because, now, he looks almost exactly like his teammate, Pit Martin, who also wears a helmet and is about the same size as Mikita.

Then there's the matter of masculine pride in *not* wearing the helmet, which still has a kind of sissy connotation to it, no matter what people say. As for me, a helmet would enclose my big ears, and when I'd go fast I'd have nothing to brake my speed and I'd go flying into the end boards!

Our club policy is to allow anyone to wear a helmet who wants to. Which is the way it should be.

On our trip to the Coast somebody remembered that December 8 was Teddy Irvine's 26th birthday. Teddy's nickname is "Fat Albert," so we composed a hymn to him. It was a two-worder. And I think I remember it. But I'd better not sing it here.

This is our first visit to Vancouver, and Francis delivered a serious talk before the game. "First of all," he said, "we've got a game in hand on Boston and we're only a point behind. So if we win tonight we'll go ahead by a point. Secondly, Vancouver is a good hockey town, so let's go out there and produce."

That we did. We produced one of the worst games of the year. Vancouver scored in the first minute and led 2–1 after the first period.

Francis ripped into us during intermission. "That was the crappiest damn first period I've even seen in my life."

I knew he was trying to make us feel bad so we'd work a little harder in the second period. And we did, but the score went to 3–1 for them. This time Francis delivered a pleasant little pep talk, and the result was a 4–1 defeat for the night. When it was over we got the big blast again.

"We're going to Los Angeles," he said, "and we're gonna get some rest, and by God we're not going to play that badly two nights in a row or else there's gonna be some hell raised."

Our hotel in L.A. has by far the best-looking stewardesses I've seen anywhere. They're from PSA, a California airline. And though we'd hoped to give "Fat Albert" a victory over Vancouver, since this had failed we let Ron Stewart select a present for Teddy.

We were gathered in the hotel lobby when Stewie spotted this gorgeous piece of PSA property.

"Teddy," Stewart said, after he'd introduced Irvine to the surprised girl, "happy birthday from us all."

How we got the business again that night at the Forum I don't understand. We had a one-goal lead in the first period with Arnie Brown controlling the puck at center ice, when a linesman actually took Arnie out of the play. That enabled Bill Flett of the Kings to skate in on me with Eddie Joyal on the other side. Flett then passed to Joyal, who passed back to Flett, who kicked the puck into the net with his skate.

Naturally, as that's illegal, I expected the referee to blow his whistle disallowing the goal, but he never did. The referee, not so incidentally, was Bob Sloan, calling another one of his horseshit games. The final was 2–2; and the defense again played pretty well. Our trouble is up front. The wingmen are not covering, so the other guys are walking in and giving those of us on defense all kinds of trouble. Francis didn't overlook this at practice the next day.

Neither had he missed something else, seemingly minor, but most important if a team expects to finish on top.

During the Kings game there was a scuffle behind the Los Angeles net, yet none of our players jumped in to help. The code is that when scuffling starts and trouble appears imminent, you've got to be there to see that things go your way. "If one guy gets pushed around," said Francis, "make sure the other team has to push *all* of you around."

Villemure can really take it. During the second period of the L.A. game, a shot deflected off Jim Neilson's stick and hit Gilles right in the throat. He went down in a heap and looked dead for a full minute, laying inert on the ice. But he was revived, went to the dressing room and returned after missing only about 40 seconds of play. When we left the ice between the second and third periods, he was having trouble talking and swallowing. Francis asked how it was.

"I'm pretty good," said Gilles, raspy and hardly audible.

Emile started laughing. "It's a good thing you don't have to sing in the choir tonight!"

We flew from Los Angeles to Oakland and beat the Golden Seals 2–1. Jack Egers scored both goals. Of course, his helmet still looks ridiculous, but maybe these goals will restore his confidence.

C-O-N-F-I-D-E-N-C-E is the most important word in an athlete's vocabulary. If you lose it, you're in big trouble. Like a rowboat without oars.

Boston is to us what the grapes were to Tantalus. They stay just out of reach by a point or two.

December 13. I came away from Oakland with a charley horse on my left thigh, so I showed up at the Garden's training room after lunch for a whirlpool bath. Then our trainer, Frank Paice, who has been with New York for 25 years, applied some liniment. It's amazing what some effective first-aid—and a good game—can do. We beat the Kings 4–0, my charley horse didn't bother me a bit and the club now has the best goals-against record in the NHL. Three days later we hung the same score on Buffalo. Two shut-outs in two games. Pretty impressive. So I suggested to Francis that it would be foolish to have a workout the following day. "After all, Emile," I pointed out, "what could we possibly practice after a pair of 4–0 wins?"

"Brad, I thought about your question all night," Francis told me the next morning at Skateland. And he gave us the works—stop and starts, two-on-one breaks, one-on-one breaks, shots on goal, everything imaginable. By the end of that workout I was really hanging.

The Cat never stops thinking about getting—and keeping—the edge on the enemy. We flew to Minnesota for a Saturday night game, and when we arrived, Francis immediately huddled us for a lecture. The topic, not new to us, was the problem of hockey player versus newspaper-man. Francis emphasized that we were *not* to divulge important team matters to reporters. "Remeber," Emile said, "reporters are simply looking for a story, and often they can hurt our cause."

He then went on about how newspapermen will take a story and twist it and turn it so that by the time it eventually appears it's something else entirely. Francis also warned us about speaking out against the opposition. "If you're going to say something about the enemy," said The Cat, "say something good. We all know that Punch Imlach likes to take quotes from the papers that are adverse to his club and hang them up in the dressing room to inspire his guys. Well, let's not have that happen to us.

"And when it comes to expansion teams, they may not be the best in the world, but they can still put up a fight. On any given night one may knock you off, so you've got to be up for every game."

We didn't take the North Stars lightly that night, though we made one cardinal mistake by Rangers' standards. We led 3–1 after two periods, but instead of maintaining a tight, defensive game we opened up our offense in the third period—something we can't afford to do—and Minnesota scored twice. True, we finally beat them 5–3, but Francis reprimanded us for not being more vigilant on defense in the last period. And he was right, especially since he was addressing our forwards. It will be interesting to see whether The Cat's defensive posture works over the long season.

December 20. Christmas is almost here and there's a friendly, festive spirit in the air, which stops the moment we get on the ice. I can personally vouch for this, because we just played Vancouver at the Garden and I had one of the biggest fights of my life, if only because my opponent was defenseman Pat Quinn, who's built along the lines of Gulliver. I wouldn't pick on Quinn if I had a choice.

It was the third period, we had a power play going and I wound up directly in front of the Vancouver net, swiping at a rebound. Quinn must have thought I was trying to chop down his goaltender, because suddenly all 6-3, 215 pounds of him came rushing at me. The first thing I knew a big leather gauntlet was flying at my face. He belted me right in the chops, leaving me either to conduct an orderly retreat or to fight back. Instinctively, I began throwing lefts and rights with my gloves off and then pulled a terrific ploy: I managed to get inside Quinn's flailing arms, locked my arm around him and then began throwing more punches. His arms are so long he couldn't get at me because I was so close to his body. Meanwhile, I kept battering away until the linesmen finally broke us up.

A few nights later in Buffalo I nearly found trouble again, this time battling an official. We were leading the Sabres 4–1 when Eddie Shack took a shot at Eddie Giacomin. Giacomin made the save, but the puck bounced to the ice a few feet in front of him. I moved right in and decided the safest thing to do would be to shove the puck under Eddie, forcing a stoppage of play, which I did.

Next thing I knew the goal judge, anticipating the puck would go into the cage, flipped on the red light, signifying a score. The goal judge insisted the puck had gone over the line, and the referee upheld his decision.

The referee, needless to say, was my old friend, Bob Sloan.

As soon as we realized Sloan was backing the goal judge, we rushed him, crowding, pushing and shoving. I myself wanted to get at the goal judge, who was separated from us by a sheet of plexiglass. If it hadn't been there I'd have broke his neck. I thought surely Sloan would hit me with a 10-minute misconduct penalty—and an automatic $25 fine—but, instead, he gave Ron Stewart the misconduct. Whatever the case, we had to argue with Sloan because that's hockey strategy. By needling the officials you soften them up for future calls, and one came a short time later.

This time we were pressing the attack around Buffalo's net when the puck skimmed near—but not across—the goal line. Though the goal judge never flashed his light, Bob Sloan suddenly ruled that it *was* over the line and a goal for us. That's called balancing the books.

We won the game 7–2 and I felt good. Emile had met with me to compare my statistics for this year and last. I was shy a point offensively, but plus 17 defensively; the best record on the club and much better than ever before. This set me up for our next game at home against Pittsburgh.

One of Pittsburgh's defensemen is Bob Blackburn, a gray-haired veteran with whom I played at Buffalo during the 1968–69 season. He's a funny guy, and Bob and I have always liked each other. Well, on this night we really were reefing the Penguins. We had them 3–0 before the first period was over, and seemed to be in their end of the rink all the time. Finally, there was a face-off at our end and Blackburn was standing directly in front of the Rangers' bench.

"Hey, Blackie," Eddie Giacomin shouted at him, "how's it going?"

Blackburn turned his head a half-circle toward us and, out of the side of his mouth, shot back, "There's a foot of snow in my end of the rink and I can't get out!"

The final was 6–1, our favor, giving us a four-game winning streak.

On Christmas Eve Gerry and I went out to visit all the

players in our Long Beach community. We did it because most of them have children and wanted to be home. Christmas day is not an easy one for professional hockey players because we often have games that night. This time, however, I was lucky and spent the day opening presents. We had a roast turkey, and then I left for the airport since we had a game in Detroit the following evening.

Flying doesn't bother me, though I know it upsets a lot of players. Gump Worsley of Minnesota quit hockey for a while because he didn't like to fly, and Carl Brewer did the same. When Phil Goyette was with us he'd chain-smoke from the beginning of a flight to the end. I figure if you're going to die you're going to die, so why not in a plane crash?

There's plenty of fooling around with the stewardesses, usually to get a peek at their legs, though when Reggie Fleming played for us he went a step further. He'd actually put on an apron and help the stewardesses serve the meals, and he did this all the time. Reggie looked pretty foolish in his tiny apron with a bit of gut hanging over it, but that never stopped him.

We arrived in Detroit fully expecting a victory, because the secret word curtailing our opponents is "dissension."

The Red Wings are having problems. Their new coach is Ned Harkness, who, after a number of successful years at Cornell University, now finds himself over the barrel. Peter Stemkowski, who played for Harkness earlier this season, says the players don't like him, that he's too severe, too much the prexy—which is not where pro hockey play-

ers are right now. Detroit has shown its unhappiness on
the scoreboard. Pittsburgh, which rarely gets more than
three goals in a game, recently beat the Red Wings 9–1;
so Detroit should be had by us.

The return to Olympia Stadium was a bit frightening
for me, as it was the first time I'd played there since my
ankle break the year before. So on Saturday, December 26,
the day of the game, I decided to go down to the arena and
clear my head.

Suited up, I skated out and went through exactly the
same moves I had gone through on the night of my accident. I skated down into the corner and around the corner.
I inspected the boards to see that everything was okay.
I then circled for a few minutes more, walked back to the
dressing room and got into my street clothes.

Yet the memory hung over me like a black cloud. I returned to the hotel and watched a football game on television, but still I kept having flashes of the accident. "You
never broke a thing in your life," I kept repeating to myself, "until that night. You never broke an arm, a wrist,
a finger, or anything." Again I felt the pain. I remembered
crawling across the ice, digging my fingers into the ice because the pain was so unbearable. Finally I got up and
went downstairs, where I ran into Garry Unger, the Red
Wing center, whom I'd played against in Junior hockey.

He did a strange thing; he confessed to me that his defensemen were having trouble getting the puck up quickly
to the forwards, and that this was hurting their club. Quite
an admission for a Detroit player to make to a New York

player; but I suspected it was accurate, because Garry was unhappy with Harkness and the whole Detroit setup.

Whatever the case, it didn't do us a damn bit of good. We led 4–2 going into the third period, but then Gordie Howe, the old master, faked a trip by Jim Neilson—Gordie took a dive over the Chief's stick—and Neilson got a two-minute penalty. A few seconds later Gordie scored. Next, Rod Gilbert lost the puck in the corner, and Detroit scored again. With a few minutes left in the game, Unger skated across our blue line and took a shot. The puck bounced off Tim Horton and right back to Unger's trailer on the play, who blew it past Giacomin. So now it was 5–4 them. The last minute we pulled Eddie, and Detroit found the open net. Thirty seconds left, and we knew we'd pretty well lost the game. The referee dropped the puck at center and bing, bing, bing—the Red Wings scored again. We lost 7–4.

This loss shook us, because we're after the best goals-against record, which would mean the first-half Vezina Trophy prize for our goalies. Now we're only one goal ahead of Chicago's Tony Esposito and Gerry Desjardins.

As we got on the bus for the airport everyone was dead silent, until suddenly Stemkowski shouted, "You guys just don't know how to lose!" I'm not quite sure what Peter meant by that, because the only way we're going to get anywhere is by winning.

The Cat really gave us hell for the game in Detroit. He laid it on the line: "You've got to play tight hockey if you're going to win, especially in the third period." And

that Sunday night we had a good chance to redeem ourselves when we took a 4–2 lead into the third period against
St. Louis.

Playing the Blues is like being victim at a woodchopper's
ball. They've got characters like Bob Plager, Noel Picard
and John Arbour, who enjoy hacking at you with their
sticks. We had our hands full. Irvine went after Bill Plager
in the first period, but Bill's older brother, Bob, rushed
over to help out; so Teddy pounded Bob. Then Jack Egers
fought Gary Sabourin; and I jumped in to grab Bill
Sutherland and one of the Plager boys. Both my arms were
busy when along comes Arbour to start throwing punches
at me.

That did it. I broke loose from the other two and said,
"Okay, Arbour, you and me, we're going out to center ice
and fight by ourselves."

Just then a linesman began wrestling me away from Arbour. He was strong and gave me a pretty rough time until the referee, Art Skov, came along.

"Since you and Arbour want to fight so badly," he said,
"go ahead. And if you don't fight I'm gonna give you both
misconducts!"

"Art," I said, "I can't fight now because I'm too tired
from wrestling your linesman." So I headed for the penalty
box.

On the way I skated past the St. Louis penalty box and
there was Bob Plager, jawing away. "Yeah, yeah, Park.
Hide behind the official!"

Let's give Bob Plager a scare, I thought. He's never won

a fight in his life. So as I passed the St. Louis box I made a fake in his direction, and Plager almost jumped out of his pads. Then I just continued skating merrily along to our box.

The Plagers gave Skov a pretty hard time. Usually when a player wants to clear the puck from his end, he'll carom it off the side boards. So when Bill Plager got the puck in his zone, Skov anticipated such a play and moved away from the boards. But instead of sending it off the boards, Plager shot it straight up center and hit Skov in the ankle. Skov immediately crumpled, then blew his whistle to halt play and limped to the sidelines waiting for the pain to pass.

"Are you going to be able to finish?" I asked as he stood near our bench.

"I'll finish," Skov answered, "if I have to stand the rest of the game at center ice."

"That might be an improvement," I said, "since you're not doing too well end to end."

Then Walt Tkaczuk chirped in. "Art, The Cat always says to skate off an injury, don't just stand there like a baby!"

Art broke up laughing at that, until he recalled the stupidity of Plager's clearing pass. "Goddamn shot. These expansion teams are minor-leaguers. Why don't they use the boards like they're supposed to?"

Later, Skov skated over to me before a face-off and said, "Y'know, Brad, when you wear number two you're not supposed to get mad at anybody."

Then Skov turned, and I saw the number two on his sweater.

Actually, I like Skov. The only referee I dislike is Sloan. Some players don't like John Ashley, but I disagree. With him, you just have to know the opposition. For example, if we play Boston, I talk to him to be sure he's in the game because the Bruins take a lot of cheap shots and Ashley will let them go unpenalized unless you keep bugging him.

We blew the 4–2 lead to St. Louis and wound up with a 4–4 tie. Our sixth game in nine days. We're dead tired. We couldn't hold the lead and that was that.

As we tromped along the rubber mat to the dressing room, I had to chuckle to myself. I remembered Emile's lecture about playing defensively in the third period. I expected it again. But when we got to the dressing room he said, "I'll see you guys at 6:15 Tuesday evening." Francis knew we were tired, so he gave us Monday off. A little break, but not as much as I'd have liked.

Driving with Jean Ratelle, we talked about how overworked NHL players get during a season. "I'd like a vacation right now," said Jean. "I'd go to Florida for a few days just to relax." Just what I'd done my last year of Junior hockey, and when I returned I played excellent hockey.

Francis could really afford to send a couple of us to Florida for a few days. Mike Robitaille was up from Omaha as a sixth defenseman, which meant there were plenty of guys on the back line; and Syl was the fourth center, so we were well-stocked down the middle.

These extra men are the "Doomsday Squad." In addition to Robitaille and Syl, there's Jim Krulicki and, sometimes, Jack Egers, none of whom play too much. Robitaille and I competed against each other in Junior hockey; he played for Kitchener while I played for the Toronto Marlboros. He was rated the best defenseman in the league then, and I was about third or fourth. Everybody thought he'd make the Rangers right off the bat.

Now he's our sixth defenseman, and the only reason he's in New York is because he can't be sent to Omaha without being placed on waivers, which means another team would pick him up for $30,000 without having to trade for him. Naturally, Mike isn't too happy about this, as nobody likes to sit on the bench. My guess is that The Cat will trade him, but for whom I don't know. We're pretty rich in all departments.

On Tuesday night, December 29, we finally got a chance to pull into first place, ahead of the Bruins. We went into the game against the Golden Seals trailing the Bruins by only one point, so a win would put us in first by a point. This factor alone should have motivated us to an exceptional performance, but the game was a complete dud.

Some people, including Francis, like to insist there's no difference between playing an expansion team and an established club, but our game against the Seals on December 29 proved there's a big one. Sure, we beat them 3–2, but we were just going through the motions, and from a spectator's viewpoint it must have been one complete blah.

It's aggravating to think how we always seem to let a

bush team like the Seals force us to play *their* disgusting style of hockey. But it's true. The reason, I think, is that teams like the Seals, Sabres, Canucks and Kings are so mediocre they run all over the ice without knowing what they're doing. And since we're trained to stay with the opposition, we go scrambling after them.

Our style is a tight, set pattern, like a well-executed football play. Each man has a job to do as the play advances up the ice, and all the established teams normally act as well as react in about the same way. But the expansion clubs get mixed up and mix us up, and that's why we wind up playing punko games like we did against the Seals.

Nothing worked out right except for one thing. My new roommate, Arnie Brown, finally scored his first goal of the season. Two seasons ago he scored 10 goals and last year he got 15, so you can imagine how hard he's been pressing. "Arnie," I said when he got back to the bench, "I'm not worried about you passing me in goals because I don't think you'll get two." That remark really upset him, but what I'm worried about is that now he has his first goal he'll be unbearable to live with.

Now the ice show comes to town and we go on a long road trip. New York, however, is right on top at the moment.

VII

A New Year, a New Season

Sorry to say, we didn't stay in first place. Boston had
two games in hand and won them both, so now they're
three points ahead of us. We moved on to Pittsburgh and
demonstrated that it's quite possible to take an early lead
and sit on it for the rest of the night. We led 3–1 going
into the last period, and went into a defensive shell like
I've never seen in my life.

The Penguins outshot us 18–2, and it seemed the ice was
tilted in our direction. I spent the night running back to
bring out the puck; only to run back again and again and
again. Now I know what Bob Blackburn meant when he
said there was a pile of snow at his end. Well, we held on
and came out with our 3–1 victory.

As I was leaving the ice, one of the Ranger press people
told me I'd been selected to go on a television program
called "Star of the Game." "Christmas," I said, "somebody
in this building must really like me." And I got $50 for
the appearance. Not bad.

On the plane an hour later, Tim Horton pops up and says, "Brad, you owe me $25."

"What for?" I asked.

"Well," he said, "you know I was supposed to go on that television show after the game, but I had to get stitched up. You went on because you were second best. And since they gave you 50 bucks, I think I deserve half of it. I just want to see what kind of a guy you are."

"Okay, Timmy," I said, fishing out $25 and handing it to him. "Now, I want to see what kind of a guy *you* are. Are you going to take it?"

"You sonofabitch," he said.

Sunday, January 3, we played the Montreal Canadiens at the Garden, and I can honestly say that it was the worst game I've ever played. Right from the start I flubbed. After three seconds had elapsed I lost the puck in the corner to Jean Beliveau, who stuck it in front and Yvan Cournoyer put it in. Fortunately, our team kept fighting back, and even though we were behind 6–5 in the last minute, we tied it up on a lucky shot by Dave Balon from behind the Canadiens' net. The puck hit the pad of their goalie, Phil Myre, and trickled by. Thank heaven, we've got next week off!

We expected to be tortured with workouts during *our* week, but instead, Francis pulled a change-up and ordered light practices. On Tuesday we had our annual East–West game in which those of us from Eastern Canada play the guys from the West. Last year we won 8–1, and this time we beat them again, 7–1. There were no real pressures.

Everyone relaxed, and for a few hours hockey was fun again.

After the game we heard the news from Detroit that Sid Abel was resigning as the Red Wings' general manager and Ned Harkness had been named to replaced him. Pete Stemkowski was surprised by the move because of how the players felt about Harkness. Peter told us that Harkness had a thing against long hair and was especially rough on Garry Unger. So one day he mailed Harkness an envelope full of hair.

Another time Stemmer wore Harkness' Cornell cap during a practice when Harkness wasn't around. Gathering the Red Wings together, he began leading a Cornell University cheer. "Gimme a C! Gimme an O! Gimme an R! . . ." Just then Harkness walked in. But Pete was cool. "Okay, Coach," he said, "they're all yours. I've got them warmed up for you!"

Stemmer didn't stop joking when he joined us. One day our scout, Steve Brklacich (pronounced Berk-la-zich) noticed that Stemkowski's name lettered across the back of his jersey carried from the far left shoulder to the far right. "Stemmer," said Steve, "you ought to shorten your name."

"That's just what I'm going to do," said Stemmer. "I've filed papers already."

"What's it going to be?" asked Brklacich.

"Joe Stemkowski," Pete replied.

Five games in eight days is no vacation. And today we got word that Syl Apps is being sent down to Omaha. He hasn't seen much ice since Stemkowski became a regular, and this will let him skate.

Losing Syl disturbed me, but we got some good news, too. Hadfield's broken hand has healed and he's due back on the starting line. Another bit of good news. I made the First All-Star Team again, with Bobby Orr. Frankly, I was surprised because I didn't think I'd played that well, but I plan to have an excellent second half.

Our road trip began in Minnesota on January 10 and we beat the North Stars 1–0. Then it was on to St. Louis, where before the game Eddie Giacomin took me aside for a bit of advice. "Brad," he said, "your shots have been too wide of the net lately. Start firing them *on goal* and you'll find they go in."

Well, the score was 1–1 in the third period and I was playing the left side when Teddy Irvine passed the puck back to me. I looked at the net, remembered what Giacomin had told me and just let the puck go as hard as I could. Past the forwards, past the defenseman, past the goal post and into the net. The final was 4–2 us.

I needed that goal because my confidence had been slipping. I'd suffered a few lapses clearing the puck, which can be fatal to a defenseman. Also, a television commercial I did for Wheaties has just been released. In it, I keep falling down and making dumb plays while the announcer repeats, "Brad, you didn't have your Wheaties!" From one end of the St. Louis Arena to the other, some jerk was yelling, "Hey, Brad, did you have your Wheaties?" Oh well, I got paid for it, and the jerk shut up when I scored.

We took a jet from St. Louis to Vancouver, where we were really out for revenge. This time we won 4–2, and I was delighted with my game. I set up the first goal for Ratelle, set up the second for Hadfield and wound up with a plus two, and a plus 26 on the season. Tops for the Rangers. Better than that, I'm managing to control the puck again; and that's the game.

From Vancouver we flew to Oakland, where we learned Carol Vadnais, the Seals' top defenseman, was out with a broken thumb and that they had several other injuries besides. Just a few nights before they'd been walloped 8–2 by St. Louis, so it figured to be an easy time.

We lost 3–1.

It was embarrassing how we performed in front of Eddie Giacomin. He's the best goalie in the NHL—there's no question about that—yet Gilles has lost only once for us and Eddie has now lost about eight times. He's damn upset because he wants to get more action but he can't because of the way Villemure is going.

To Chicago for a Sunday afternoon network television game, where believe it or not we led 3–0 in the first period —and ended up losing the game 4–3. So that finished our road trip, three out of five. Not bad, except that we blew two games, which is not good for a top club.

On Monday night we had the All-Star banquet and I found myself sitting between Gordie Howe and Bobby Orr, with Bobby Hull across the way. I felt funny talking to such great players, and the thought of Gordie Howe or Bobby Orr or Bobby Hull listening to Brad Park struck me as absurd. It was also strange greeting opponents left and right just like they were old friends.

Making the All-Star team does more than fill your heart with pride; it also helps fill your pockets with money. Since I've made the team, people recognize me, even in New York. I've been asked to do commercials and to endorse products such as table hockey games. Except now I'm beginning to worry somewhat about all these endorsements. With the Wheaties commercial and the Sher-Wood hockey stick commercial and the Canada Dry soda commercial, people may get tired of my face. But in the meantime I'm enjoying my new-found popularity.

From time to time I've asked myself, "What's the difference between an All-Star team member and the good players who are not on the team? What makes a superstar?" I think there are three factors. First, the player must have some natural talent. Secondly, he must be able to utilize that natural talent to its potential; he must go out on the ice and try hard. Finally, the player must have something special inside—character.

Gordie Howe, Bobby Orr and Eddie Giacomin are my leading superstars. I don't consider myself a superstar yet. I'm a good hockey player who will stand out if certain things break my way.

The banquet itself was pleasant enough except for Stafford Smythe, president of the Toronto Maple Leafs, who was sitting on the dais behind us with the other NHL governors. He kept making wisecracks—all in poor taste— even during the presentations. His comments were so brutal that I'd rather not relate them. Suffice to say, they were appreciated by none of us.

Smythe was eventually asked to present the Conn Smythe Trophy, named after his father, which goes to the star of the playoffs. This year Bobby Orr was the recipient. Stafford struggled down the steps to make the presentation, smiled for a photographer and then turned and said, "Bobby, tell the folks how I signed you when you were 14 years old."

Orr was terribly embarrassed, but he simply smiled and acted like a gentleman.

As for the All-Star game, each player on the winning side gets $500 and the losers $250. "I can assure you," Bobby Hull told me, "that the West will come out of it with $500 in each guy's pocket."

"No way," I said.

After the banquet I had a few beers with Harry Sinden, who'd led Boston to the Stanley Cup in 1970 and then retired. He's quite a man, and it's hockey's loss he quit the Bruins. Harry, I understand, really got along with his players, not only as a coach but as a friend. If Francis ever decides to leave coaching, I'd like to see Sinden get the New York job. He'd fit in perfectly.

I'm sure Harry still misses the camaraderie, the fun and friendship of a hockey team. Those outside find it hard to understand. I know my wife does. I'll go off with the guys for a few beers in the afternoon and then come home and she'll say, "Why do you do this?" My answer is simple. It's because I have a good time. I enjoy it.

Harry's successor is Tom Johnson, who never coached before in his life, although he's a member of the Hockey Hall of Fame. Johnson was lucky in a way. He inherited a well-set team. All he has to do now is stand behind the bench and send the men over. But he's got a few discipline problems. And one is Sanderson.

The Bruins would like to get rid of Sanderson because he's a disturber; he opens his mouth when he shouldn't. In fact, like a small boat in distress, he ought to shape up.

Lately, he seems to be doing a little less disturbing and playing better hockey. Maybe Derek learned a lesson. Last year in the playoffs Eddie told Derek to keep his head up, "or we're gonna get you." That kind of warning has to penetrate, because he figures there are 18 guys on the other team who want to get him. So he begins to have second thoughts. Then, I'm sure, Derek took a look around the league and figured there were about 240 *other* guys who'd like to get him. That's a lot of players, and big odds against Sanderson.

Of course Derek is lucky, because the Bruins are so loaded they take the heat off him. And Phil Esposito is lucky there's a Bobby Orr on his team. Sure Esposito gets his goals, but he gets them against Buffalo, Vancouver, Pittsburgh, Philadelphia and Los Angeles, not against clubs like ours. Can you imagine how little he'd score if he played the Rangers 14 times a year? And Montreal? And Chicago? Why, he'd starve.

Which is not to detract from Boston. They have a fine hockey club. But I don't go along with Gordie Howe. He has said that the Bruins are better than the Rangers because of Orr and Esposito. My answer to Mr. Howe is, "What happens if one of those two gets hurt?" Its not wise to build a team around two guys, because if you lose one the club is in trouble. By contrast, we can lose one or two players and not worry a bit about collapsing. Toronto won the Stanley Cup four times in less than 10 years without All-Stars.

The Boston style is to hit you all the time; they hit you as you pick up the puck, when you make a pass, after you throw a pass, all the time! There's only one way to cope with that, and that's to turn around just as you're about to be hit and give the Bruin six inches of stick. I don't like butcher hockey, but sometimes the Bruins make it impossible to play any other way. Particularly Sanderson and McKenzie.

Orr, for all his talent, doesn't like to be hit. So we must try to hit him, cleanly of course. Except, damn it, he's hard to catch. But I know that when he's hit he gets upset and his game is thrown off.

One of the myths of hockey is that Bobby Orr is unstoppable. Some people have written, and rightly so, that Orr can be held in tow by forechecking him in his own end of the rink before he has a chance to get up a head of steam, and by taking advantage of the big openings he leaves when he takes off on one of his many rushes into enemy territory.

Another myth about Orr is that he's a gentlemanly and clean player. Actually, Orr can be a hatchetman just like some of his Boston teammates. It bugs me to see him do that because he doesn't have to revert to the cheap stuff in order to succeed. But he may, and this makes the opponents more wary of him. Sometimes Bobby pulls off cheap shots that really aren't necessary under any conditions.

A good example of how Orr gets thrown by hard body contact was the time when Pat Quinn nailed him with a terrific check right in Boston Garden—a good, clean check—and Orr couldn't take it. He spent the rest of the playoffs running at Quinn.

My point is that Bobby Orr, like the rest of us who earn our living playing hockey, is human, and I had an opportunity to observe this first-hand as Orr's teammate the next night in the All-Star game.

I opened the game on defense with Orr, and it was curious to play in Boston Garden with nobody throwing objects at me, and even an occasional cheer *for* me.

On the very first shift Chico Maki of the West got the puck and skated in on Orr and myself. Suddenly Red Berenson of the West cut between us, and it appeared that Maki would pass to Berenson. At that moment Yvan Cournoyer yelled from our bench, "Shoot! Shoot!" Maki shot and scored. So once again, for the second year in a row, the first shot on Eddie Giacomin was a goal.

One shift later Hull fanned on a shot, but it bounced off Eddie's pads and into the net. Well, as I'd been on the ice for both goals too, I skated over and said, "Okay, Eddie, the pressure's off. Now let's play." However, the game itself was boring and lackadaisical, not unusual for an All-Star contest. Everybody on our team seemed to be going the wrong way; and as we'd never played together, hadn't even practiced together, there was no beautiful hockey and the spectators were disappointed. No doubt a number came expecting to see one star carry the puck through the entire opposition and score. But when everyone is almost equally good that's pretty difficult.

On top of that the All-Star game was scheduled for Tuesday night, and a number of teams, the Rangers included, had games to play the following Wednesday and Thursday nights. Now this is just dumb planning—or is it greed?—on the part of the owners. There should be a schedule break at All-Star time, and the players should be allowed a few scrimmages together so we can mesh our styles and give the fans something to see. What stupidity!

The tight schedule showed the next two nights. First we had to battle like hell to tie Philadelphia 3–3 on Rod Gilbert's goal with 19 seconds remaining. Then we tied Buffalo 5–5, once again on Gilbert's two late goals. Francis was pretty ticked at our defense. But some credit must go to Gilbert Perreault, the Sabres' big rookie. Granted, the kid likes to skate with the puck and he's not looking to share it, yet he must ask himself, "Who am I going to pass to on this lousy club?"

We took Minnesota 6–2 on Sunday. So now it's those damn Bruins again.

Francis is concentrating on solid checking and body contact. Getting "hits"—body contact with the opposition—in the other guy's end of the rink. The pressure is really building for that Wednesday game against Boston. Half of New York is fired up, and here I am still working at it.

Johnny McKenzie, the pesty Bruin winger, has a separated shoulder and will be out for several weeks. Dear John, I'm sorry. . . . We'll put Stemkowski out to stop Phil Esposito, and without McKenzie, the Bruins' Stanfield line should be nullified, which will put the Sanderson line against Jean Ratelle's line. So, we're balanced off nicely, except for Bobby Orr. Well, we'll just have to keep him covered, though he's got to be the fastest guy in the league.

I'm still having some problems handling the puck, but they're not that bad. Defensively, however, I'm playing the puck more than I should. I must play the man, for that's how I'm being beaten on defense. During the past few days I've tried to think aggressive. I'm going to have to be mean and get some respect out there. I did that my first two years in the NHL, but I've shied away from it lately and people have taken advantage of me, so I'll have to get back in the old groove.

En route to the dressing room on Wednesday, January 27, a strange thing happened. Actually it was a pretty routine walk until I opened the dressing room door and saw Frank Paice helping Glen Sather into a new pair of skates. "What the hell is goin' on here?" I said to myself. "Sather is with Pittsburgh. Since when are we outfitting the Penguins?"

So I walked over and asked, "What are you doing here?"

Sather smiled that big, broad grin of his and replied: "Guess what? I got traded. To the Rangers."

"You're kidding. For whom?"

Then he dropped the bombshell, and told me that Francis had swapped my buddy, Syl Apps. I felt like a fool. My pal got traded from my own team and I didn't even know about it until I walked into the dressing room.

Walter Tkaczuk was jubilant. When he saw Sather and found out what had happened, he shouted, "Hey, geez, is that ever great!"

I couldn't believe Walter. "Why? What's so great about it?" I asked.

"Well," Walter explained, "Syl is a center and he's gone. So that means Stemmer and Ratty and me don't have to worry about a fourth center taking our jobs away."

"Walter," I said, "don't you realize that Sather plays center, too?"

Aside from my friendship for Apps, the trade inspired other thoughts. Some good, some bad. Sather will help our club; he's rough and can kill penalties. I'm sorry Syl's gone, but he wanted to play regularly and now he'll get that chance at Pittsburgh.

Sather played well for us that night against the Bruins, but we tied. New York played a tight-checking game without any rough stuff, because Boston wanted to skate. It's interesting that we adapt our style to suit their play. Maybe we should start taking the lead, and challenge the opposition to play our game for a change.

Jean Ratelle squared things for us with a close-in shot

late in the third period, and the game ended at 2–2. This left us three points behind Boston, except the Bruins still have that key game in hand on us.

Syl scored a goal and an assist that night in his debut with Pittsburgh. The Penguins beat Toronto 3–1.

After the Bruins, the Flyers clobbered us 5–2, and I was on the ice for four goals against. Awful. Then we tied the Kings 2–2. Worse. Pretty soon something's gotta give.

VIII

Rebuilding the Rangers

Monday, February 1, we dealt Arnie Brown, Mike Robitaille and an Omaha kid named Tom Miller to the Red Wings for veteran forward Bruce MacGregor and Larry Brown, the defenseman who started the season with us.

The deal shocked me. Brownie and I had been roommates on the road for a long time, and now, all of a sudden, he's going to Detroit. I think I'll miss him even more than Syl.

When I was a raw rookie coming up to the Rangers, Arnie was an established veteran. To me he represented the foundation of this hockey club. He was established. He had come up to New York when the club wasn't doing well, and he'd improved with the team until the Rangers were a contender. Then, all of a sudden, he's gone!

I wonder what Francis is thinking. A year ago we were in first place, going along well, and had a good team. Then, trades. Same thing this year. It shakes the team up, and it's not all for the good, either.

On Monday night we held our little farewell for Arnie. I went to his house with Jim Neilson and Rod Seiling, and we sat around trying to figure the trade. Nobody could.

Beyond the fact that we all recognize we're nothing more than pawns in this hockey game, to be sold or traded at will, Arnie had contributed a lot to the Rangers. Still, none of this meant a damn. It didn't matter that Arnie had scored a club record in goals for a defenseman the previous year, or that he'd been a key factor in the transformation of the Rangers. When there was a little dealing to be done, he was simply a piece of property. Period.

These days hockey players are beginning to question "the System." I think many of us now feel that you've got to milk the hockey cow for all you can get, and then go back for more. Granted, one feels greedy, but the player is merely responding to an atmosphere created by the league itself, which has expanded everything as much as it could and as fast as it could. And so now we, too, are out after every dollar available.

All things considered, however, we're still not such a lousy bunch. And one of my favorite people, right from the start, has been Eddie Giacomin, who's the constant butt for our Italian jokes because of that thin film of olive oil that surrounds him in the goal crease.

Then there's Tim Horton, who still gets fun out of hockey after 20 years as a pro. Tim is a very strong man, so his alias is Superman. "Are you looking for a telephone booth to change in, Clark?" is a typical line we throw at him.

We call Larry Brown "Wood" because he said so little his first year with the club until he had a few drinks under his belt. Rod Gilbert, our classy veteran, is "Rody," after a girl from Thailand named Arunee, his rather steady date for a year or two. Bob Nevin is simply "Nevvy," while Bill Fairbairn is "Dog," short for "Bulldog" after the persistent way he goes digging for the puck.

Vic Hadfield, the club's practical joker, is always phoning somebody to imitate a sportswriter or opposition manager, and to pretend a trade has just been made. He's "Wicky." And Ron Stewart is simply "Stewie."

Jim Neilson is "the Chief" because he's an Indian; but we also call him "Tony" because his middle name is Anthony. Rod Seiling is "Sod," a combination of Seiling and Rod and a way of separating him from Rod Gilbert.

Dave Balon, a pretty funny fellow, is called "Bozy," from Bozo the Clown. One of his idiosyncracies is to order a beer, and when it arrives he puts salt on his arm, then licks the salt and has a sip of beer. And so on. And whenever we're in a restaurant and find a small packet of salt, we'll say, "Hey, save this for Bozy."

Balon really gets on the nerves of opposition players. I found this out in practice, where he's always nattering at the fellows he's playing against. He's a little guy and cuts wide to the left, making him hard to catch. On top of that, he's so bowlegged that it looks like he's riding an elephant instead of skating.

Walt Tkaczuk is always kidded about his last name. To make it simple we just call him "Walter." His name is correctly pronounced "KA-chook," but many on the team mispronounce it "TAY-chuk." But he doesn't get upset about this any more often than he gets stood on end in a game. In short, I don't remember the time.

Our straight-arrow is Jean Ratelle, known affectionately as "Rat-ty." He is, without doubt, the model hockey player; totally dedicated to the sport and the team. Jean's problem is sleeping after a game. Following a particularly tough one on the road, some of the boys may go out for a few beers and in the morning look like hell. But Jean will look worse because he's been working all night, trying to sleep.

Jean plays hockey according to the rulebook. He would never think of elbowing or slashing a guy or doing anything really physical; he's just a beautiful player. He and Gilbert, good friends since their junior days in Guelph, will usually room together on the road. And Jean keeps Rod under control. He'll say, "Hey, Rod, there'll be no girls in the room after 9:30 P.M. No girls!" And Rod will say, "Fine," and that's that. Jean is so straight I bet he won't even drink champagne out of the Stanley Cup.

Jack Egers is "Smokey," not for his hard shot but because he's always puffing on a cigarette. He lacks stamina and has to be really mad before he's effective. When he's mean, however, he's a good hockey player.

Teddy Irvine has also improved as he's gotten tougher.

That "Fat Albert" tag—he's the hero of a Bill Cosby sketch—came when Teddy walked into a restaurant one evening not long after he'd been traded to New York from Los Angeles and announced for all to hear, "Hey, hey, hey, boys, here's Fat Albert." The name fits because though Teddy has very thin legs, he's pretty heavy round the top.

From time to time Francis has called up Ab DeMarco, the tall young defenseman from Omaha. Like Giacomin, DeMarco is of Italian descent. "Ab," Eddie will say, "you and I have to stick together because we're the only Italians on the club." Then he'll add, "But remember, I'm the only *regular* and I'm the best-looking."

Ethnic jokes are commonplace in the locker room, and, as you can imagine, Pete Stemkowski is the butt of his share of Polack stories, none of which bears repeating here.

By the same token there's occasional needling between the English- and French-speaking players on the team. Gilbert and Ratelle are kiddingly known as "Pepsis" or "Frogs," Canadian nicknames for the French. On a few teams—Philadelphia and Montreal, for example—there have even been problems in this area. Vic Stasiuk, the Flyers' coach, actually prohibited Andre Lacroix and Serge Bernier from talking French on the ice. Ridiculous.

The Rangers don't really have a club leader in the sense that Montreal has Jean Beliveau or Boston has Bobby Orr. True, Nevin is the captain, but he hasn't the perennial goal-scoring abilities of a Beliveau or an Orr, or a Gordie

Howe for that matter. Though Nevvy is the best guy on the team for the job.

Francis prefers a team style with a capital T. We pull together, no matter who gets the goals or how many. We're taught to be unselfish. Everybody is like a brother, and we all, presumably, like each other. Francis is an idealist. He doesn't want his players to disagree, and in that sense he's a dreamer. We're human beings, so we're bound to have disagreements. Some guys on this team are not real pals. But once we step on the ice, everybody wearing the Ranger jersey is my buddy. You have to believe in every guy on the team if you're going to have a winner. So now I welcomed Glen Sather and Bruce MacGregor to the team. Sather is "Slats," a carry-over from his Pittsburgh days, and MacGregor kept "Murdock," a nickname he acquired in Detroit.

The Sather deal looked good after we tied Boston, but MacGregor began slow. We got beaten 4–2 by the Black Hawks in his debut, ending our home winning streak. Even worse, we're now eight points behind the Bruins, who still have a game in hand. We're not playing the close-checking hockey we must in order to win.

On Thursday afternoon, February 4, the defensemen met with Francis in our Detroit hotel before that night's game against Arnie and the Red Wings. We decided the defensemen were not getting their shots through from the point, and that the forwards were not standing in front of the enemy net to deflect shots and screen the goalie and look for rebounds.

But we came away from the meeting with a feeling of unity. Francis, always thinking of defense, stressed that we shouldn't be so goal-hungry. "Play defense," he said. "Get the puck out of your end. Put it in their end. But don't go running after it, taking unnecessary chances. Then we'll start winning some hockey games."

And that night, against a team crippled with injuries up and down the line, we did manage a 1–0 victory on Rod Gilbert's goal. The surprise was Bruce MacGregor, who, until then, I hadn't considered a particular asset to the club. As we were both on the right side, I got a chance to observe his remarkably steady play, up and down the wing, and the job he does checking.

Bruce and Larry Brown were fascinating dinner companions the next evening, as the two of them spun stories about the Red Wings under Ned Harkness. At Christmastime, according to MacGregor, the players were so upset they held a team meeting and decided unanimously that Harkness was driving them nuts and that he must leave. But how to get him out?

They approached Al Eagleson, advisor to the NHL Players' Association, to act as their liaison with owner Bruce Norris. And though he agreed, nothing came of it. Instead, Harkness was named general manager of the club and Sid Abel was fired. According to Bruce, that really shook the players. So now the man they have no respect for is in overall charge.

Yet, I wonder. Harkness has sure been working hard as general manager. He traded Garry Unger and Wayne Connelly to St. Louis for Red Berenson and Tim Ecclestone. If he continues to make trades like that, Ned Harkness will come out smelling like roses.

I was sorry to learn that Harry Howell had been sold by the Seals to Los Angeles for straight cash. Harry was the senior Ranger when I came up, and he helped me as much as anybody, and taught me a lot. He was also a fine gentleman and a real competitor. Now why Charlie Finley, the Seals' owner, should sell such a player for cash, I can't imagine. Unless it's Harry's high salary. But even so, Harry is worth every cent of it.

On Saturday, February 6, we beat Vancouver 5–4 on their ice as Dave Balon scored his 32d goal to lead the team. But the big thing was that Billy Fairbairn saw some ice and came off with two goals. It's funny how things change: A year ago Billy was a candiate for rookie-of-the-year honors, and this season he's been a forgotten man.

We held a practice Monday to prepare for the next night's game in Boston. Strangely enough, Francis didn't handle the workout, and I'm not sure why. Maybe he felt he tightened us up too much before our last game with Boston. Whatever the case, Ron Stewart ran the scrimmage in a somewhat peculiar manner.

"If you guys practice too hard," he warned us, "I'll send you *off* the ice." So a pleasant limbering-up skate for tomorrow's "four-pointer."

For a while it looked like we'd take the Bruins. We had a 3–2 lead when Horton was called on a questionable tripping infraction. Boston tied the game, then went on to win when Wayne Cashman whacked one in from the side of the crease with about ten minutes remaining. I thought Gilles Villemure had trapped the puck long enough between his pads and the goal post for referee Art Skov to blow his whistle. But there was no whistle, and Cashman poked it into the net.

Francis pulled Gilles with a minute left, but Boston scored into the open net, and then Orr got another goal. So we came off the game with a 6–3 loss. And yet we played well enough for 59 out of the 60 minutes to have won.

The way they pass out assists in Boston is something. Bobby Orr scored the Bruins' first goal when he stole the puck from Ratelle and went in alone on Villemure. It should have been an unassisted goal since Orr did the job alone. Instead, the Boston official scorer gave assists to Phil Esposito and Ken Hodge. *They never even touched the puck.*

There have been a rash of colds the last few days. Giacomin has been out for more than a week and is depressed, which means Gilles will continue playing goal for us. The games are getting tougher now as everybody is fighting for a playoff berth. The playoffs are the whole season for a skater, because that's where he makes his money. And that's where the glory is, too. And when you're a professional athlete, that's what you think about. Fame and fortune.

By the same token, the whole thing can be a real pain in the ass as well. On Friday, February 12, we had a practice at Skateland and, since it was Lincoln's Birthday, there must have been about 800 people there. After the workout some 70-odd kids were waiting out by our cars for autographs. Now, I don't mind signing autographs because I remember chasing after players like Max Bentley and Teeder Kennedy of the Toronto Maple Leafs for their signatures a few years back. But on this day the kids came running up to me, pushing and shoving and sticking their pens in my face: "Sign this, sign that!" until it really got on my nerves. So after I'd signed about 40 slips of paper, I said. "Listen, I'm goin' home. That's all for now." Damn, I hate rude kids.

The average fan, however, really isn't a problem, but there are enough weirdos in the audience on any given night to make life miserable both on *and* off the ice. New York has one of the worst in a skinny blonde who's been hounding the players for years. Whenever a single guy joins the team she goes after him like a starlet after her producer. But when the guy cuts her off she becomes obnoxious at games. She stands right next to the boards during practices, yelling obscenities at the players she doesn't like, me included. Except, whenever I meet her off the ice, she walks up with a big smile and says, "Hi, Brad, great game you played."

Another fan will take advantage of you when you're going good. One night just such a man fell into conversation with my wife. And when he discovered who she was, he said he could get clothing for her at a reduced rate. She gave him our phone number. Two nights later he phoned and said he was coming over with some clothes, and he arrived an hour later. He had brought along a new vest for my wife, and proceeded to chew my ear off. The next day he phoned. "How's your wife enjoying the vest?" And then, "Geez, Brad, I hate to bother you, but I need tickets for Sunday." I told him I was sorry.

New York has one advantage over Toronto. In New York a hockey player can pretty much get lost in the crowd and enjoy a degree of privacy that isn't possible in a city like Toronto, where every hockey player is recognized. After a game at the Garden, my wife and I can take off and spend the rest of the evening in a restaurant without ever being recognized. Rough on the ego, but it relaxes the nerves.

With single players the problem is "groupies," girls—not particularly attractive ones—who chase them just like they chase after rock groups and basketball and baseball players.

Another bunch who get on my nerves are the Boston Garden fans. Enough said. But while on the subject of Boston, it appears Ted Green is back to his old tricks. Dirty hockey. In our last go at Boston, Green high-sticked little Dave Balon; then, when Dave was down, Green kicked him. It's a good thing I wasn't out there. I'd have chased that clown right off the ice.

But Green's act didn't end there. In the second period he and Stemkowski were chasing after the puck on an icing call, and Green got to the puck first. Just then Stemkowski brushed him, and Green took a couple of big swipes at Stemmer for no apparent reason.

I wonder what could possibly be going through Green's head. Perhaps it's just that he's back in Boston Garden, his zoo, and he wants to show the animals he's the same old Teddy. However, it's people like Green who give hockey a bad name. Quite simply, he can't be trusted. He swings at players with his stick, and that stick is always up. So, one of these days, I suspect he'll be swung at again.

Our club was trying to put on a brave front as we mucked through February. Somehow we couldn't get untracked. We lost 2–1 in St. Louis, and then just barely beat the Blues at home the next night. Next the Canadiens beat us 3–0 in the Forum, a night of total embarrassment for Gilles and me.

The score was 2–0 for them and we were still very much in the game when a Montreal player shot the puck out of his end, down toward our goal. I could have picked it up and skated behind our net, but suddenly Villemure was out of his net and racing for the puck. "Gilly," I yelled, "shoot it down the ice!"

He heard me and he shot. But Gilly didn't lift the puck high enough. It hit Jacques Lemaire in the skate, and he plopped it into the empty net. Gilly was 30 feet out at the time.

Also that night, defenseman Guy Lapointe really creamed me. His check was a beauty. Up in the air like a rocket; then down on my head like a bomb. But a surprising hip bruise was the most painful upshot of that collision. And a bruised hip makes it almost impossible for a skater to overextend himself, which he must do so often when racing for the puck.

On the bright side. Eddie Giacomin, recovered from his virus attack, returned to the nets Saturday, February 20, at Pittsburgh. We were terrible. But Eddie, not to be denied, won the game 2–0. In fact, he played so well that there were times during the game when I wanted to hug him. His shutout gets him a $100 bonus from Francis, which means he'll stand us a round of beers. A shutout is strong tonic for a goaltender, particularly one who's been depressed for a while. Walter Tkaczuk scored one of the goals and I got the assist on it; we each received the offensive bonus promised by Francis at the start of the season.

When we came home from Pittsburgh I ran into Tim Ecclestone, who'd been traded by the Blues to the Red Wings along with Red Berenson. Being friends, we closed for a beer and some solid talk. Timmy then told me his version of the story behind that trade.

He felt the swap had nothing to do with Berenson and Ecclestone's ice play. Instead, it was made because both were active in our union, the NHL Players Association. Scotty Bowman, the Blues' manager, and Sid Salomon, Jr., the club owner, took a dim view of Berenson heading the association. And Tim had been elected player representative of the Blues, and Salomon was down on him for *that*. "I hated to leave St. Louis," Tim told me. And who could blame him, or Red for that matter? They were the team's two leading scorers. But they crossed management, and got the ax.

Though Tim and Red have stabilized the Red Wings, Giacomin beat Detroit. So on to Philadelphia and the Flyers, a team we haven't beaten in two years. But we extracted a 4–2 win, then went on to beat the Penguins 4–0.

Curious game. My old buddy, Syl, got into a fight with one of our men, and I couldn't decide who I was rooting for. Apps took the fight and, in so doing, finished off my Ranger companion for the rest of the game. Later on, Neilson and MacGregor collided and Jim went down. Instinctively, I knew something was wrong, and when I raced over to see what, Jim's eyes were fluttering crazily like a man going into convulsions.

Right away I knew he had swallowed his tongue. By this time Frank Paice was out on the ice, but, without any help, Jim's tongue came up and everything was okay again. A sigh of relief. But unfortunately for Jim the news wasn't all good. He's gone to the hospital for further examination of his knee, and it appears some emergency recalls may have to be made.

Our troubles were just beginning. We took the plane back to New York for a game against Vancouver, which was a disaster for me. The ice was atrocious. Because of some flaw in the pipes, the surface was soft in spots. This can ruin the game as well as cripple a player. Still, there was a game to be played.

The score was 2–2 in the second period when I started a rush from our end. As their defenseman Pat Quinn came out, I cut hard to my right. Suddenly my skates went out from under me—I'd hit a soft spot, and was decidedly down. Pat Quinn, who was right on my tail, then fell on my left knee with all his 215 pounds. The two of us skidded along toward the end boards in a messy heap.

"Are you okay?" Quinn asked.

I was in such pain I couldn't even answer. My knee had popped twice and I wasn't able to move. Meanwhile, play continued, and Nevin took the puck and scored, putting us ahead 3–2. Then out came Frank.

"What's wrong?" he asked.

"My knee," I said. But as I limped off, my legs suddenly felt okay. I did a few knee bends and they still felt pretty good. So I went to the dressing room and put some ice on the knee.

The third period, although I took one shift on the ice and we scored, was a mistake. The knee really hurt. When I got to the bench I said, "I'm not going to finish this game, 'cause if we can't beat a team like Vancouver with a two-goal lead, then the hell with it."

We did. And my injury was diagnosed as stretched ligaments on the inside of my knee. Naturally, I began thinking that exactly a year ago I had broken my ankle and missed the last month of the season. This time it was my knee. I wondered how the knee would be in March and early April when it came time for the playoffs. My fingers were crossed.

IX

View from the Sidelines

March 1, a Monday, I went to see team physician Dr. James Nicholas about my knee. And this time I got the word—out of action two or three weeks. "I'm going to California," he said. "I'll be back next Sunday. Don't do a thing until I return."

The words fell like a ton of bricks. I'd hated to miss part of last season, and now I'm out again. Dr. Nicholas told me to go to the hospital where a doctor would drain the fluid from my knee. So I phoned Francis to tell him the news.

"I figured that," he said. "Now, look, as far as the press or anybody else is concerned, you're out Wednesday, *but you'll be back for the weekend!*"

For a moment I couldn't figure it. What was this all about? Dr. Nicholas said I was to be out two or three weeks, and now Francis wants me to say I'll be ready by the weekend. Who's kidding whom?

"Here's the reason," Francis said. "You're out for two to three weeks. Rod Seiling's out for two to three weeks. And with the race going the way it's going, we'll have to make a trade for a defenseman."

Francis was thinking. If the papers printed the truth about my injury, the opposition would know we're in deep trouble, defensively, and they'd be much more difficult to trade with than if they thought we were pretty well set on defense.

I doubt whether Emile really fooled anyone. At a press conference soon afterward somebody asked him if he was going to send me to Florida to recover.

"Yeah," he snapped. "I'm goin' to buy him a sunlamp!"

That night I began figuring who the next trade would involve. I knew Francis couldn't get anyone from a club still in the race. So he had to trade with teams like Buffalo, Vancouver, Detroit, Los Angeles or Oakland—where there simply isn't much defensive talent.

Two possibilities. One is Oakland's Carol Vadnais, who could help us, except that he's been hurt a lot this year. The other is a big, steady defenseman on Detroit named Dale Rolfe, who hasn't played much this year even though he was the Red Wings' best defenseman last year. To me, those are the only two possibilities. So now to see who Francis goes for.

One of my first projects during the long lull after the accident was to answer my fan mail. And as I sat to do so, I remembered an incident that had occurred one night the year before, after a game with the Bruins.

A fellow approached me and said that his son was sick in the hospital. He was a small man, Italian, modestly dressed. His son was about to undergo an operation and he wondered if I'd take the time to stay hello to the boy. I said I would. Meanwhile, I gave him a few pictures of myself to give his son, whose name was Thomas.

Sometime later I received a letter. "Dear Mr. Park. I want to thank you for the pictures. My son, Thomas, wanted to thank you in person. We went to the Bruins' game and waited for you but you went down the elevator so fast after the game we never got to see you up close. Thomas never really enjoyed the game until he watched you. We would appreciate it if you could find the time to come to our house for an Italian dinner.

"My son has a rare bone disease. He now has 24 tumors on all joints of his body. He lives a normal life but he has pain. He has had three major operations and he has to have a lot more. He is a very good and brave boy. His one love now is hockey, especially you. If you can't make it for dinner we would appreciate it if you could see him in the hospital as he soon will have another operation. Good luck for the Stanley Cup. God be with you and your team. Thank you. Mrs. DeBlasio."

The letter upset me, hearing about all the problems the boy was having, so I decided to phone him. "Hello, Thomas, this is Brad Park." But even though I talked to him for five minutes, he didn't really understand who I was.

Later that month I received another letter from the DeBlasios, which began: "Dear Mr. Park. I'm writing for my son, Thomas. He is dictating this letter. 'Brad, I'm so sorry I didn't know it was you on the phone yesterday.' We took Thomas to the doctor, who said he has new tumors and that they'll have to operate. In the meantime he plays hockey on skates, even though he's not supposed to play, and pretends that he's you. He just wants to be a hockey player. We know he will never be able to be a professional but it's just a joy to see him try. He doesn't give up and I wonder why." The letter was again signed by Mrs. DeBlasio.

I now have a photo of Thomas, and his lucky penny is taped inside my hockey pants. And it's for such reasons I always answer my fan mail.

While I was sidelined I would watch the team from the stands. Wednesday, March 3, we beat Oakland 8–1. Bruce MacGregor picked up three goals and two assists. And it was no joy missing a game like that, as we all yearn for the game in which we can coast.

My next experience on the sidelines was Saturday night, March 6, watching the Rangers play Detroit on television. We blew a 2–1 lead in the final minute of the game and came off with a 2–2 tie, while I twitched and jerked myself into a state of complete exhaustion.

I tried to relax the way the doctor ordered, but no luck. I'm sure to drive myself and Gerry nuts before I get back in action. The next best thing is to stay as close to the players as possible; to at least *feel* a part of the team if I can't actually skate with them.

Sunday we had a home game against the Kings, who carried a 2–1 lead into the third period. During the intermission I went to our dressing room and sat down beside Irvine. "Jesus Christ, Teddy," I said, "you've got to get going and knock some guys down out there."

Well, the third period began and Irvine went out and picked up the puck from Bruce MacGregor on a scramble in front of the net and rammed it home to tie the game.

A few minutes later Stemkowski knocked Harry Howell off the puck and passed it to Irvine, who beat goalie Denis DeJordy, making it 3–2 for us. With a minute to go the Kings put out an extra skater and yanked DeJordy. The face-off was in our end, and Larry Regan, the Kings' coach, did something that makes one wonder just what goes through the minds of those guys behind the bench.

He put Ralph Backstrom on at the right point where a defenseman would normally stand. Backstrom is a left-hand shot, so it was plain stupid to put him on the right side because it meant that when the puck came to him he'd almost certainly have to take it on his backhand and then waste time getting the puck to his forehand for the good shot.

Sure enough, Los Angeles won the face-off and the puck was pulled to Backstrom on his backhand side. Then, just as he tried to switch the puck to his shooting side, Irvine rushed him, intercepted the puck and fired it into the empty net for his hat trick.

My sideline attitude is different now than it was last year when I was injured. Gerry has noticed it, too. Last year I was ornery, depressed, always down. This year I'm excited watching the games or listening to them on radio, feeling very much with it. But last year I was worried because the team kept losing, and I was afraid we'd miss the playoffs. This year I'm feeling up because I know we'll at least finish in second place. The team's losing streak last year when I was out must have been just a coincidence. The club is playing well now, and I couldn't be happier.

Still my knee hasn't responded as I'd hoped it would, so I won't be able to start skating until March 16. Poor Gerry.

When I examine the NHL race, I find the most interesting battle is between Montreal and Toronto *not* to finish third. Montreal has third now, which means the Canadiens would meet Boston in the opening playoff round. No team wants to do that. Interestingly, both teams are losing a lot nowadays. There's just no real incentive to win, I guess.

I persuaded the doctor to let me try skating a day early. My leg felt weak but there was no pain. So the following day I worked out with the team.

On the sidelines you miss the humor of the dressing room, the hotel lobby and the ice. I remember a silly incident that happened earlier in the season. Perfectly meaningless, but it will serve to recall the good times players have together.

Walter and I were sitting in a restaurant having a few

beers when Walter lifted his mug, not realizing it was full. A good bit of the beer spilled onto his trousers. "How could you do a thing like that?" I asked him. He stared at me with that blank look of his, then replied, "It's easy. All you have to do is miss your mouth!"

Our dryest humorist is Jimmy Neilson. One night Egers had the puck on a two-on-one break, with Ratelle in perfect position to get the pass. Egers banked the puck off the sideboards and lost it. Neilson, on the bench at the time, commented, "Well, at least Jack played it right."

"What do you mean 'played it right'?" I asked.

"At least," said Neilson, "the boards give the puck back to you."

Not long after that, Hadfield was on the receiving end of a good line. Vic was the only one back, with no goalie, when the opposition attacked with three forwards. A pretty impossible play, but as the three guys moved in, Bob Nevin, yelled from the bench the best advice possible: "Spread out, Vic, spread out!"

The layoff left me a half-step behind my teammates. Rod and I worked together when Francis sent three-man forward lines skating in on two defensemen. We both could tell that our reflexes had dulled, which meant we'd have to play defense relying more on our experience than our speed. And I looked to Rod to take more of the experience load.

Still the leg keeps paining, and there's been fluid on the knee. I'm favoring the good leg too much, and even though

I'm not right Francis wants me to accompany the team to Philadelphia for our game against the Flyers on Thursday, March 18.

That same afternoon, Francis had Rod and me on the ice, working our asses off until we couldn't move. It was torturous. And I was further annoyed because the leg was still very weak and I couldn't turn. At times I even fell to the ice, but he kept us slaving away.

I'm worried about the weakened leg, because its condition has deteriorated and I'm compensating by shifting all my strength to the right leg. Perhaps I should get some weights and start lifting them to strengthen the injured leg.

It appears the final standings in the East are just about set. Boston is first and we're second, with Montreal third and Toronto fourth.

It's going on 30 years since the Rangers finished in first place, which is by far the worst record of any established team. And so the question: What kept us from first? We got enough points to guarantee first place any other season. It was just that Boston had a fantastic year. A break here or there and we might have caught them. But they have more points, and the main reason they have more points is Bobby Orr.

Phil Esposito didn't hurt us much. He only had two goals against us in six games. And we split our season series with Boston. So the only other explanation is that we didn't win the games we should have.

Pressure could be a final reason. We are the only New York team not to have won a championship since World

War II. The Yankees have. The football Giants have. The
Jets have. The Mets have. Even the Knicks have. And we
think about that as we wonder when our turn will come.

On March 18 the Canadiens beat the Leafs 4–1 in Montreal, and Clarence Campbell, it seems, made a fool of
himself after the game was over.

Peter Mahovlich, I read, bowled over Toronto goalie
Bernie Parent, and while Parent was down, Canadien
defenseman Guy Lapointe shot the puck into the empty
net. Instead of ruling "no goal" because Parent had been
knocked over by Mahovlich, Friday allowed the score.
Campbell was sitting near the Toronto bench at the time
and apparently Jim Gregory, the Leafs' manager, and
John McLellan, Toronto's coach, had a few choice words
to say about Referee Friday. Once the game was over,
Campbell gave Friday hell for his non-call. Campbell
yelled so loud that even the newspapermen outside the
referee's locker room could hear him.

This was Campbell's mistake. It's not his job to worry
about officials. He has Scotty Morrison, the referee-in-chief,
to do that. So what if a referee does make a bad call; it's
not intentional. Referees are bound to make mistakes from
time to time—even Bob Sloan. So now Friday looks like
a goat because of Campbell's blunder.

We're rapidly moving toward the end of the season and
I'm really worried. Francis plans to skate us every day,
and my leg has been bothering me. It's not strong, it hurts,
and my puck control is off as well.

Many weeks have passed since Jean, Vic, Walter and I had our dispute with Francis. He's been absolutely fair with us ever since. For now, at least, the episode involving Pro Sports is a thing of the past.

Emile is able to distinguish between his coaching and managing jobs. The last ended the moment we signed our contracts, when he was immediately our coach again.

But this doesn't mean *I've* forgotten everything. Not by a long shot. I'm going to discuss the new contract with Emile sometime after the season is over, and this time I'll have my attorney, Larry Rauch, along. Still, I think this season's left Emile with a little more respect for me than he had before.

I certainly respect him as a worker. Even on our plane flights he sits alone up front, his attaché case spread on his lap, going over statistics and business—trying to make trades, seeking to better the club, always working.

Francis has a good hockey mind. The other day when I told him I was a little concerned about my play, he suggested that when I get the puck at the blue line I should fire it instead of looking for someone to pass to. "I'm not getting the number of shots-on-goal I got last year," I said.

"That's simple," he explained. "They're covering you a lot closer now. You're an All-Star defenseman."

He's right. I have to move around a little bit more to get in the open. The opposition isn't giving me as much room or time to unload. So I've got to make my own time.

Another thing I like. We have curfews but Francis rarely

checks us on them. He doesn't bother us in the back of
the plane, and he doesn't go looking for trouble. But when
it comes he can handle it. If we have an 11 o'clock curfew
he assumes we'll honor it on the grounds that breaking
curfew is a serious matter with him. "You can fool around
and get caught once. But if you get caught twice, you're
gone."

He's got faith in us and he expects this to be returned.
He'll never cut a player apart in front of the press. When
a player does something wrong he'll attempt to cheer him.
"He's got a lot of composure," Bruce MacGregor said after
we got badly beaten one night and The Cat said nothing.
"Some coaches would have gone right down the line and
let everybody have it."

I wonder how long Francis can do both jobs. He gave
up coaching once, when Boomer Geoffrion took over, and
I'm convinced he'll give it up again because of the strain.
He works as many as 14 hours a day, and no matter how
strong a man is, that's a long day. But The Cat wants the
Stanley Cup more than anything, and I think he'll keep
doing both jobs until he wins it.

Francis has helped create a feeling of unity among the
players. Of course, he'd like everybody on the team to be
equal, right down to earning the same salaries. He'd like
to avoid all jealousy among the players. And this isn't
easy, because you're dealing with some pretty charged people.

Inevitably, there are players on the team with more

talent and more personality than others. Francis allows this —to a point. However, were a particular player ever to consider himself more important than the team, something would be done to correct the situation.

This happened with Mike Walton and the Maple Leafs. He was more interested in having a good time than worrying about his team. He fought with management far beyond reason. Finally the Leafs dealt him to Boston. It had to happen because when management is trying to group a bunch of guys together to perform as a team and one of the guys fights them, he has to go.

March 23. We beat the Sabres 6–2 to clinch second place. A distinct improvement over our fourth-place finish last year. This means we each receive $1,250 as a bonus from the league. If we win the first round of the playoffs, we get an additional $2,250; and $1,500 if we don't. It's the same in the second round. Winners of the final get $3,000; losers, $1,500. So if we go all the way, we can make $8,750 per man.

Lifting weights with my knees has begun to pay off. When I was a Junior hockey player and injured my knees, weight lifting did the trick. And now it's working once again. I am turning with some ease for the first time since my comeback, but the real test will be this weekend when we play a home-and-home against Boston.

Having clinched first place, the Bruins slipped into a slump. They lost to Buffalo—of all teams—at home, and then to Chicago. Tom Johnson has been resting Bobby Orr lately in preparation for the playoffs, and without Orr

the Bruins are just another team. This was proven in our
weekend doubleheader. Saturday night, with Orr on the
sidelines, we whipped the Bruins 6–3; they were never in
the game from the start.

Boston has good forwards, but they have to be set in
motion out of their own end, otherwise they're nothing.
That's where Orr comes in. He controls the puck, and
therefore he controls the game. With Orr gone we were
able to pressure Boston's defense and keep the puck in
their end.

One of the Boston players told Walter Tkaczuk that the
Bruins hadn't had a regular practice *in two months!* And
that all their workouts are optional and not all the players
have been showing up.

Boston's philosophy is score-score-score, with a minimum accent on defense. This is a rather undisciplined
approach and could prove disastrous during the Cup
rounds when the defense plays tight and the checking is
close. The Bruins have the mistaken notion that they can
just turn on the power and turn it off whenever they
please, but we proved them wrong in the second game of
our weekend series.

Before the game I spoke to Orr. "Listen, Bobby," I said,
"if you keep sitting on the bench, I'm goin' to catch you
in scoring. All I need is 90 more points!"

We beat Boston 2–1, and the Bruins acted like a bunch
of spoiled children. Wayne Cashman and Phil Esposito
slamming their sticks on the ice. The goals just aren't

coming. They need Orr to untrack them. And maybe even he won't be able to do it. Poor Boston.

Our primary concern now is winning the Vezina Trophy for Giacomin and Villemure. We have a game against Chicago March 31 and an eight-goal lead over their goalies, Esposito and Desjardins, who won the Vezina last year.

Fortunately we managed to hang one on Chicago by a 4–2 score before being routed by Montreal 7–2. The same night of our appalling exhibition at the Forum, however, Chicago won 4–1 over Detroit, cutting our Vezina lead to four on the final day of the season—when we'd face the Red Wings at the Garden while the Black Hawks went against Toronto at home.

The team in our dressing room prior to the final regular-season game was on edge. We had been dreadful against the Canadiens, but, even worse, we'd jeopardized the Vezina for our goalies.

So with everybody's nerves at the breaking point, we resorted to humor. And soon the needles were darting. The hope, of course, was to relax Giacomin, our goalie for the finale.

When we lined up for shots, Eddie was tight as a drum. Right away the word passed around, "Stay out, stay out on Eddie," meaning that we should shoot from far out so as to give him a better chance of stopping the shots, and restore his confidence.

But even that didn't help. I shot an easy one from the blue line—about 40 feet—and he waved his stick at it and it went in. I shot three more and he fanned on two of them. It was the same with everyone else. They'd toss the easiest shots at him and they'd go in. Soon the fans were booing him, and Eddie got even more nervous.

I began wondering whether Francis should have started Villemure. It was a difficult decision. Gilles really had come along well during the season. He fooled a lot of people who didn't think he had the goods—including me. I remember the first time I ever saw him; he walked into the dressing room and I looked up and saw this little guy with a pot belly and a brush-cut and thought he was a scout. I couldn't believe he was a hockey player. Even after I played with him in that first training camp and later at Buffalo, I didn't think he was of major-league caliber. But I was wrong. True, he can't handle his stick like Eddie, who is a master at firing the puck off the boards or passing it to a defenseman. However, we concentrate more when Gilles is in the nets, and this, in turn, helps the club. Also, Villemure doesn't take so many reckless chances around the net; he's always falling on the puck, which gives us a breather. But Eddie was going to be our goal-tender, and deserved to be.

The Red Wings were relaxed. They opened up the game, but we stayed tight on defense, as we have all season.

The first period we panicked but came out ahead 1–0. Every time the puck came into our end we just shot it out like a dead mouse. By the time the second period began we'd shed all our jitters and really laid it on. The final was 6–0. Eddie got his eighth shutout of the season. We won the Vezina and, more important, we played tight hockey when the chips were down.

X

The Playoffs

Monday, April 5. Francis had us on the ice for a relatively light skate to keep us sharp without tiring us out. He has to be careful because we have our first two games on Wednesday and Thursday nights at home and then again on Saturday and Sunday at Toronto. That's four big ones in five nights, which is a lot of hockey.

Francis gave us a second brisk workout on Tuesday, and extra playoff precautions have been taken. The press and spectators are banned from our workouts, so that we can restructure a few things in private. These were largely a matter of firming lines and making a few emergency plans in case anything goes wrong. And there was the psychological factor as well. We mustn't forget that the playoffs are important.

A valid concept up to a point. But Francis, I believe, took it a bit too far. A woman reporter from the Toronto *Daily Star* wanted to interview a few of the wives. Francis said they shouldn't talk to her, that it might prove distracting. So Gerry, and the wives of Jean and Walter, refused her. But Tim Horton's wife, Lori, simply laughed at the edict. She not only gave the reporter an interview but also posed for pictures at the Garden wearing hot pants. And of course The Cat didn't do a thing.

During the scrimmage Francis elaborated on the weaknesses of Toronto's two goalies, Bernie Parent and Jacques Plante. And by the time he was through, I wondered how they'd ever made it to the NHL.

The Leafs have two excellent centers in Dave Keon and Norm Ullman, but we can match them with Ratelle and Tkaczuk. Our edge is on the third line, where Stemkowski should outplay Jim Harrison or Darryl Sittler.

Also, we're opening the series at home. The last two years we've opened on the road, which makes you nervous and jittery. You can't relax at all. Being home, however, you go through your normal routine and it's like any ordinary home game.

The way I see it, we'll win our series in five or six games. Boston will take Montreal in five or six—the Bruins beat the Canadiens 7–2 in their final regular-season game on Sunday—while Chicago should sweep four straight from Philadelphia. As for the St. Louis–Minnesota series, I like the Blues in six.

Our opening game with Toronto didn't quite go according to plan, although perhaps I'm not the best reference point because in the second period I took one of the hardest bumps I've ever received in my life.

The guy who delivered the blow—it was more like getting hit by a bus—was Toronto's tough rookie forward Billy MacMillan. Frankly, I'm not exactly sure how he hit me. I was at center ice when the next thing I knew—whack!—either his knee or stick caught me in the head, and I was knocked cold.

When I regained consciousness I couldn't remember playing the first two periods. And though bits and pieces of the action slowly began coming back to mind, they didn't seem to have anything to do with me.

Of the third period, I remember Francis taking it a bit easy with me; not putting me on the ice quite so often. I kept trying to play my normal game, but the reflexes weren't there. And when I tried to concentrate—"Get back in the game, Brad," I'd tell myself, "get back in the game!" —I knew I was merely going through the motions.

I kept slipping into groggy spells. But I wasn't making any mistakes, and I was concerned that if I pulled myself off the ice in the middle of a Stanley Cup game, Emile might think I was a quitter.

When the final buzzer sounded, I looked around—at the rink, at the scoreboard, at the penalty benches—and asked myself, "What in hell were you doing out there?" And to this day I don't know.

We were lucky. Toronto outplayed us but we got a break late in the second period when Nevin's shot caromed off Baun's leg for a goal. And we rallied in the third to come away with a 5–4 win, and a 1–0 lead in the series.

On Thursday I felt lousy from the neck up; I lay down, hoping the pain and fuzziness would disappear by game time. But that evening we were all like bit players in *The*

Comedy of Errors. The Maple Leafs kept taking the puck away from us, and won 4–1.

In the third period, however, we had a real time of it. Jimmy Harrison, the big Toronto center, hit Vic from behind, and Vic came around swinging. Not far away I got involved with Darryl Sittler in a tugging match. I grabbed his sweater, pulling it over his head.

I really had no intention of getting into a full-scale fight, but I did want to rough Sittler up a bit. Just then referee Lloyd Gilmour, who's a pretty tough egg, came over and said, "Okay, you two guys—break it up! You've got five-minute penalties now."

That didn't bother me since the game was nearly over, so I just kept giving it to Sittler. "All right," said Gilmour, "now you've got ten."

Well, that got me mad and I was ready to give it to Sittler some more when Gilmour piped up, "Lookit, you guys, either you let go or I'm going to throw you the hell outa this game—*and you'll miss the rest of this series.*"

I immediately released Sittler, skated over to Gilmour and put my arm around his shoulders. A pretty funny-looking vignette.

"Now look, Lloyd," I said as calmly as possible, "take it easy. Let's not get excited about this." Meanwhile Sittler was standing there in complete amazement. And Gilmour was just as astonished. He didn't say a word. And for that little misdemeanor, I received a ten-minute misconduct in addition to the five minutes for fighting.

That, however, was just the start of things. Parent, Toronto's goalie, had skated over and grabbed Vic. Vic retaliated by tossing Bernie's face mask into the crowd, where it passed from spectator to spectator until it finally disappeared. Meanwhile, not to be outdone, Giacomin had rushed from his end of the rink to tackle Parent.

Since Parent's mask was gone and he didn't have a replacement for it, Bernie refused to continue, so Jacques Plante took over. When the dust had cleared, Vic was out of the game and I was in the penalty box.

The next thing I knew there was a fight between Teddy Irvine and Jim Dorey and another between Glen Sather and Ron Ellis. Then Jacques Plante dashed out to join the fight and, once again, Giacomin took off from his end. At this point Rickey Ley and Jim McKenny leaped off the Toronto bench and headed for the brawl. And before their skates hit the ice, I was on my way.

By this time everybody was on the ice throwing punches. Somebody pulled my sweater over my head, and the next instant I was squaring off with Brian Spencer. We weren't throwing punches; we were wrestling.

"Spencer," I shouted, "you're wacky. You haven't got a brain. You'll never make it as a hockey player."

Finally we were separated, and I was ejected from the game. In addition I collected $250 worth of fines—$50 for the misconduct, $100 for the game misconduct and $100 for coming off the bench.

Well, anyway, as you may recall, Toronto won the game 4–1, tying the series at one apiece. The Leafs played outstanding hockey. And as for the fights, they were simply a product of frustration. The guys who are fighting for Toronto—Harrison, Spencer—are the same ones who never put the puck in the net. You don't see Dave Keon, Paul Henderson or Norm Ullman pulling that nonsense.

Friday at Skateland I discovered that a lot of us were tired. Such fighting and wrestling as the second game contained really rips the crap right out of you. Your arms feel so heavy you think you have weights attached to them. A few guys were just stiff and sore, while others were out-and-out sick. Francis wasn't sympathetic. He sounded like the overseer of a chain gang. "Now, look," he said. "I don't give a good damn about your little hurts. We have to get together. Regroup. Go back at them again. There's no reason to miss practices or to try to get out of them. Now let's start again!"

So off to Toronto for game three.

Saturday I bumped into Jim Gregory, my Junior manager, at Maple Leaf Gardens. I did a double take because there was something about him that reminded me of the old Marlboro days. Then it came.

"Hey, Jim," I said, "you haven't changed since I played for you."

"What do you mean?" he asked.

"Well, when you use to get on a winning streak you didn't shave, and it looks like you've got something going there now."

He felt his beard and laughed.

At Saturday's meeting we agreed that on the power play if our right wing or left wing took out the Toronto defenseman this would produce an important opening for us. And that night it worked—up to a point.

Except, plain and simple, we weren't "up" for the game. Toronto won 3–1. That's two straight losses, and morale is very low. What are we doing wrong? And how is Toronto beating us? It was decided to hold another meeting before tomorrow's game.

After the loss I went out for a beer with my parents. Just tried to relax a little.

Sunday we decided that on the power play we'd just shoot the puck into the corner where our forwards will be skating, and that we'd check Toronto and keep the Leafs in their own end, forcing the younger players to make mistakes. We felt that would win for us. And it did.

Early in the game we got a big save from Ed Giacomin on Dave Keon, and came back to score on a goal by Bob Nevin. By the third period it was 4–0. The Leafs scored twice, but we never gave them a chance to tie the game. So we have a two-out-of-three series, with two of the games on home ice.

We were pretty relaxed returning on our charter flight from Toronto, but I'm not myself. I'm still a little gun-shy since MacMillan dropped me in the first game. I keep saying, "You've got to break out of it; you've got to break out of it." But the change doesn't come easy.

Tuesday, April 13. A good one for us. Teddy Irvine scored early and Vic Hadfield got one in the second period. We were checking the Leafs at every turn, and Nevin made it 3–0 in the third. Then, suddenly, we found ourselves two men short on penalties. But Rolfe and Horton played exceptionally well during the first minute, and then Seiling and I went out for the second shift.

Sittler took a shot for Toronto that was deflected into the net by Jim McKenny, whose stick was illegally above his shoulder at the time. Yet Ron Wicks ruled it a goal, and the game ended 3–1 in our favor.

During the game Francis used six defensemen, and I was skating quite a bit with Larry Brown. I wasn't happy because I didn't get as much ice time as usual, but we have the edge now and I think it's almost over.

On the afternoon of the sixth game I was at Maple Leaf Gardens again, so who do I run into but Jim Gregory. I was sitting at the Gardens' coffee shop when Gregory walked in. A second double take. And he knew why, too.

"Hey, Jim," I said, "you've shaved." He interpreted the remark just the way I thought he would. I was suggesting we'd knock off Toronto that night. And I don't think he appreciated my crack one bit.

If we contain the Leafs for a period or so, then the pressure will revert to them. They'll open up, and we can exploit their openings.

Jacques Plante started in the nets and the score was 0–0 well into the second period, when Walter knocked the puck away from Jim McKenny at center ice and skated in with a clear three-on-none breakaway. The only man back was Plante. A 1,000–1 shot. Walter moved right in on

Plante. Jacques made the save; except he couldn't control the rebound, which bounced right out to Nevin. And Bobby gave us a 1–0 lead.

It stayed that way until well into the third period. Francis wasn't giving me any ice time and I didn't know why. Then, with less than three minutes left, the Leafs started moving toward the New York zone. And Francis called for a line change as they attacked, which gave Jim McKenny of Toronto just the room he needed. He fired a shot just over Giacomin's shoulder to tie the score and send the game into sudden-death overtime.

That goal might have killed us, but, depressed as we were, we didn't wilt in the overtime. We checked and checked and held Toronto as the minutes ticked away. Then, at about the nine-minute mark, Francis put me on the ice with Jim Neilson.

Gary Monahan of the Leafs fired a slapshot across the crease about a foot high. It went over McMillan's stick, then swung around the boards where it took a funny bounce. Mike Pelyk, a Leaf defenseman playing on left point at the time, rushed in to trap the puck, but he missed it. Nevin stole the puck and broke away, with Hadfield on his left. A two-on-one break, with me following right behind in case there was a rebound.

As Nevin moved in on Plante he faked a pass to his left, then shot the puck along the ice to Plante's stick side, his right. It zipped across the goal line . . . and we'd won the first round!

Cheered by our victory we headed for Chicago, worried

only about a possible letdown. Francis is happy because it's the first time he's taken a team past the first round. And to celebrate, Emile put us through a light workout on Saturday, April 18, in preparation for our first semi-final game Sunday night.

That afternoon every one of us watched the seventh game of the Boston–Montreal series on television. Naturally, I was rooting for Montreal. After all, I'd once lived there; the Canadiens are a classy team; and I hate the Bruins.

The Bruins took a 1–0 lead before their home crowd. But the Canadiens never folded. They took the play to Boston and forced the Bruins into mistakes. They tied the score, and then went ahead. Montreal tied up Bobby Orr. Boston panicked. Phil Esposito did nothing. And Montreal won.

At Chicago Stadium I went through my usual pre-game routine. I sat on the bench, taping my sticks; I put on a garter belt, jock and underwear, shin pads and socks; then I just sat there taking deep breaths. Fifteen minutes before our warm-up I tied the laces on my boots, taped my pads, hoisted the suspenders of my pants over my shoulder guards, adjusted the elbow guards, put on the blue jersey. Lastly, I slapped some Vaseline on my face, because I'd shaved earlier and didn't want to get a sweat burn, and combed my hair. All of which took just fifteen minutes.

Chicago scored first. It was a cheap goal, as Pat Stapleton's power-play shot from the blue line hit Jimmy Neilson and bounced into our net. The score stayed that way until late in the third period, when I gathered the puck behind our net and sent it ahead to Gilbert. The second I did that I spurted toward the Chicago zone with Hadfield. As Rod hit the blue line he passed to Vic, while I broke for the net. Hadfield saw me and tried a pass, but the puck went straight to Esposito, who worked to cover it.

A split-second before he grabbed the puck, I kicked the rubber out across the net to where Ratelle had moved. With just under four minutes left, we tied the score. And we held them until the end of regulation time.

We came out for the first sudden-death period and—poof!—just like that it was over. MacGregor sent the puck from behind Chicago's net out to Stemkowski, who fired a screened shot past Esposito. With 1:37 gone on the clock, it was over and we felt unbelievably happy.

The second game of the series was on Tuesday. Our only concern was a cut Eddie Giacomin suffered on his glove hand, stopping a shot by Bobby Hull. Of course, with Eddie you never expect him *not* to play, he's such a great competitor. The cut was 1½ inches wide and open, because he'd refused to have it stitched until after the second period.

Eddie was still somewhat bothered by his hand Tuesday night, so we fully expected Francis to start Villemure. But Emile fooled us and went with Giacomin.

Cliff Koroll got the first goal for Chicago, shoveling the puck through Eddie's pads after a scramble in front of the net. Still we continued to play tight hockey, until midway

through the second period Dennis Hull and Koroll caught
us on a two-on-one break. Koroll fed Hull a perfect pass,
and he beat Eddie with a shot to the upper corner. We
didn't panic, except we couldn't score. And at this point
I felt we should have opened up. But we didn't. Francis
finally pulled Giacomin with less than a minute to go, and
Dennis Hull put the puck into the empty net: 3–0.

We left the ice totally depressed. We hadn't played well
and we knew it. There was no faulting Eddie. He played
a good game; we just didn't get him any goals. But we did
win the odd away game. Now, if we win our three games
at home we'll be laughing!

On Wednesday, April 21, Francis called an optional
practice and I didn't show up. Only about five guys made
it. The others took the day for rest and rehabiliation before the two big Garden games Thursday night and Sunday afternoon.

This time we came out flying, even though the Garden
ice was lousy. Vic scored a hat trick, and we beat the
Hawks 4–1. Vic had predicted after the opener we'd take
them four straight. Cracks like that can be dangerous. But
this time we played so well we really felt unstoppable.
Chicago looks ready to fold, and Coach Billy Reay flew
them home after Thursday night's game. And neither did
we return to Manhattan until Saturday night, when we
holed up at the Penn-Garden, across the street from Madison Square.

Francis showed us the films of Thursday's game, and
I'm not playing All-Star hockey. Perhaps I'm still a little

afraid after that MacMillan check. Also, Francis is using three pairs of defensemen, which has cut down on my ice time and hurt my play.

The fourth game, Sunday, April 25, was the CBS "Game of the Week" and began at 2:05 P.M. Players have mixed reactions about playing in the afternoon; some say it disturbs their normal equilibrium.

Well, on this particular day we didn't play at all. Chicago outchecked and outskated us, and held a 4–0 lead at the end of two periods.

Between the second and third periods Francis really tore into us—particularly because we'd abandoned his favorite tight-checking pattern.

"Even though you're down a couple of goals," he shouted, "there's no need to open the game. We've got to play our style. Now let's go out and show them what's what."

Fourteen seconds into period three, Chicago scored again.

Nothing went right. A bit later I hit Pit Martin at our blue line and lost my stick. Suddenly Francis came to mind. "Always go for your stick if the puck is in your end of the rink," he'd said. Okay. The puck *was* in our end. I went to get my stick, Larry Brown lost the puck, and Chico Maki scored. The final was 7–1, Chicago.

If that wasn't bad enough, Walter suffered a twisted knee in the first period which bothered him in the second, and half-way through the third he was taken to the hospital for an examination.

We left for Chicago Monday afternoon and, fortunately, Walter was with us. Francis gave us a very firm
command for this game. "We're not going to open up,"
he insisted. "We're going to send one forechecker into
their zone throughout the game and have two guys coming back. We're going to play *tight hockey. Very tight
hockey!*"

That's just what we did. Even though Chicago took a
2–0 lead, we came back in the second period to tie the
game, and then held them scoreless in the third. So into
sudden death once more.

At 6:35 of the first overtime there was a face-off to the
right of Giacomin. Pit Martin of Chicago went up against
Walter Tkaczuk. Martin won the draw cleanly, skimming
the puck back to Bobby Hull. In one smooth motion Hull
flung it at Giacomin. That was it. We lost 3–2. Down three
games to two, with the sixth game scheduled for Madison
Square Garden.

Usually, at this stage, a club will feel out of contention,
but not us. We believe we'll beat them in New York and
wrap up the series in Chicago. We need a big score in the
sixth game to give us confidence and deflate them.

The sixth game, on Thursday, April 29, was a classic.
Again we fell behind 2–0, and all of a sudden it looked like
the last game of the season. But then Rod Gilbert got our
first goal, and we still clung to our tight-checking game
while outplaying them.

We tied the game early in the third period before the
end of regulation time. But we couldn't get the tie-breaker.

So it was sudden death once more. A goal for them and it's summer vacation; a goal for us and we force a seventh game in Chicago on Sunday afternoon.

Our strategy wasn't profound; we just had to make sure the Black Hawks didn't get the next goal. I thought we had it wrapped up when Vic beat Tony Esposito, but his shot bounced off the goal post and out of danger. Several Hawks also had good chances in that first overtime. Yet Eddie held fast, and the period ended without a score.

Early in the second overtime, Stan Mikita came down on a two-on-one with Dennis Hull and fired a high shot that glanced off Eddie's mask. Eddie went down and we thought he was hurt. Everybody sort of hesitated for a minute. But he got right back up. Mikita then passed to Bill White coming up from the slot. He shot, hitting the left post, and it came to Stan, who fired, hitting the other post. I'll tell you, everybody on our bench was blessing themselves.

The dressing room was deadly silent between the second and third overtimes. The word was: "Don't give 'em a thing—play it tight." We were tired. Every so often I'd get a flashback of Mikita and White and bless myself again. Then the oxygen arrived and several of us took whiffs. It smelled like ether.

When I hit the ice for the third overtime my nerves were dulled. The mental stress was terrific, and I was getting more tired by the second. In fact, I was so tired I could easily have entertained the thought of quitting, giving up, going home.

Then, it happened. Just before a Chicago penalty had expired, we stormed into the Black Hawk zone. Pete Stemkowski, Teddy Irvine and Glen Sather. Irvine took the first shot and Esposito saved, but Stemmer moved right in and banged home the rebound. It was over!

"'Way to go! 'Way to go!" was about all anybody could say. I dropped my stick and gloves near the bench. "Just one more and we're on our way," someone shouted. We all walked over to Stemmer and shook his hand, and then Eddie's hand, and then anybody's hand that was available. Francis walked in and shook everybody's hand. "This is our finest hour," he said.

"The big one is Sunday," Stemmer muttered, perhaps more significantly.

XI

Chicago, Chicago

The momentum we developed from our sudden-death victory was unbelievable. We were cocky. We were certain to take the seventh game. We'd outplay them; we'd outskate them; we'd outshoot them. We were stronger and in better condition. We had a better passing attack, better goaltending, better defense. We'd win. No question.

Saturday night, May 1. Rod Gilbert and I decided to go over to The Palmer House and catch Paul Anka's act. Paul, who's from Ottawa, has one hell of a voice, with a personality to match.

While Anka performed, something occurred to me. He was telling us about the time he appeared in the film *The Longest Day* and how he wrote the title song for that movie. Then he sang the song, and I can't remember ever listening to an entertainer sing with more feeling. Tomorrow, Sunday, was going to be *my* longest day. I was right.

When I tried to fall asleep that night, I tossed and turned for hours trying to project how the game would develop. It was early morning before I finally conked out, and we had to be up by 10:30 A.M. because the seventh game was in the afternoon for the benefit of television.

When I got to the dressing room every guy was thinking positive, and this feeling persisted through our warm-up. My own legs felt rubbery at first, but I was raring to go. "Brad," I said to myself, "there's nothing beyond this— unless you win."

Nevertheless, Chicago went ahead 1–0 on a power-play goal by Jim Pappin in the first period. But we came back right away on a goal by Stemkowski, our overtime hero. So it was 1–1 at the end of the first period.

In the second period we were determined to go out and get that first goal. And that's just what we did. Vic tipped the puck to Gilbert, and Rod drove it home: 2–1. We figured we had the series in the bag.

After the face-off, play swung down to our end. Bill White, their defenseman, skated across our blue line. He faked to the right and tried to go to his left. He tripped on that maneuver and fell a few inches from Hadfield's stick. Vic never touched him, but referee John Ashley called Hadfield for tripping. "Ashley, you slob!" I shouted. "What a horseshit penalty that is."

With the momentum we had, I wasn't really worried. Actually, we did a pretty good job of killing the penalty, until Bobby Hull took a shot at Giacomin from just inside the blue line. Eddie stopped it on his pads all right, except he couldn't control the rebound. So he skated with it, trying to jab the puck out of danger. But as Eddie was attempting to clear the puck, Cliff Koroll zeroed in on him. The puck hit Koroll in the shin pads and bounced right back into the net. Now it was 2–2. Still fine. "The Black Hawks aren't going to beat us," I said to myself. "No sweat."

At the start of the third we were still raring to go. This was it. The last period. In our minds there was no way the game would go into overtime.

We played textbook hockey at the opening of that period. The checking was excellent; the forwards went up and down their wings just as Francis wanted.

And then it happened.

The puck came to me and I skated up to the red line before firing it into Chicago territory. I deliberately carried it *over* the center red line, because I knew that if I didn't I'd be called on an icing and the face-off would be deep in our territory. Precisely what we didn't want at this stage of the game. Just then I saw the linesman's hand shoot up in the air to signal an icing call. Oh, hell! Either I'd goofed or the linesman had, but it was too late to run it again.

The face-off was at our end with Walter going up against Lou Angotti, the Black Hawks' little utility player. Actually, Angotti shouldn't have been there, except Pit Martin had been hurt and Angotti was in as his pinch-hitter. What happened in the next few seconds will stay with me for some years to come.

Angotti won the face-off like a magician. That easy. He then put the puck directly on Bobby Hull's stick and

Hull, standing to Angotti's right, let the puck go as it touched his stick.

Hull had previously taken one good shot at Giacomin in the entire series. And this had come in the identical manner. That's a one-in-a-million chance. All season long I haven't seen a face-off draw go back as cleanly as it went back to Hull on those two chances. The puck was in the net like a shot, and Chicago was ahead 3–2.

We kept fighting. We were all over Tony Esposito in the Chicago net. We had our chances, but we couldn't put it in. Then Francis yanked Giacomin, and Chico Maki scored into our empty net. And it was all over.

When it's over you know it's over. The Black Hawks lined up for the traditional handshaking, though a few of our guys were so depressed they went straight to the dressing room. I shook hands, however. I didn't feel like it, but it's the custom. When I got to Bobby Hull, I said, "Beat the Frogs. Don't let Montreal win the Cup!"

I must have sat for 20 minutes on my bench in the locker room staring at the floor. "It's hard to believe," I thought to myself. "Eight months, and now it's all over. What kind of nonsense is this? Is this any way to treat a hockey player who loves the game and wants to play?"

Then I began thinking about the winning goal. Could it have been prevented? Of course, there was the icing call. Against me. Damn. But maybe our forwards might have gotten in front of Hull's shot. No. Everything happened too fast. Yet the puck had to go past four players before it got to Giacomin: Hull's own man, the left and right wings and the defenseman on that side. Like threading a needle. The odds against Hull were terrific because in addition he had to beat our goalie. And he'd done it—twice! My God!

Chicago's God. "This is the last time I'll be taking off my equipment," I thought. "No more practices, no more planes. That's it." I felt like a man climbing a peak, but not being able to quite reach the top. Suspended.

Francis passed around thanking us. And when I saw the expression on his face my stomach spun. He'd followed us every step of the way from September into May. He was convinced we were going to win the Cup, and he was the guy who had put us together. He'd worked harder than anybody. And all the disappointments in the world were on that man's face.

As I watched Emile go from player to player, I felt that if I'd only known how this defeat would crush him I would somehow have put six pucks into the Chicago net all by myself.

Francis finally left to talk to the reporters, and Tim Horton turned to me. "I've played a few years and I've had many happy experiences in this room and many sad ones, but this has got to be the saddest." And it was the same for 20 other guys.

The best team had not won. People will say, "Wait till next year," but who cares about next year? *This* was supposed to be it for the Rangers.

The shock of defeat still gripped us as we climbed aboard the bus for the airport. And the ride was a quiet one. "Hey, it's over," we were all thinking. But nobody talked about it. Then it was on the plane, and a few guys opened a bottle or two and beer started flowing and we loosened up a bit. Still, nobody wanted to talk about the game. We made small talk about vacations. Nobody had mentioned vacations before.

At Kennedy Airport we got a big lift. It was amazing. About 3,000 fans had come out to greet us.

On Monday I went to say good-bye to Emile. As I rode up in the Garden elevator I thought back to September and all last summer's problems. The holdout hurt because I didn't jump off on the right foot. I wasn't in shape and it was tough trying to play catch-up with my body. Still, I'd had a better year than the one before. My offense was better and my defense was better. The team had more points—we scored more goals and we set all kinds of team records.

But still we should have done better. And as I shook hands with Emile, I knew that he felt the same way.

It took five days for the season to begin to wear off. Gerry and I spent a week in the Bahamas, and then we returned to Toronto where we've bought a house. I was anxious to see how the annual NHL draft would develop, particularly because I hoped Tim Horton would be back with us in 1971–72. But New York didn't protect Tim and Pittsburgh claimed him. The Rangers will miss that guy. And so will I.

On top of that Nevin has been traded to Minnesota for

Bobby Rousseau. That really was a shocker to him; and we all felt it happened rather abruptly.

Bobby deserved a better farewell than that. Here was a fellow who'd been the team captain, who'd joined the club when it was horseshit and helped lift it to a playoff berth for five straight years. Surely his farewell might have been administered with a touch of grace. But how do you say good-bye gracefully?

The final spring crusher was the NHL All-Star team. I wound up in a tie for second place on the First Team with J. C. Tremblay of the Canadiens. But since he got more first-place votes, I was dropped to the Second Team.

Tremblay deserved it, and in a way I'm glad he got it. Because now I'm convinced that next year it won't even be close. It will be Orr and Park once more.

A Postscript

On Thursday, May 27, I read the headline: "Jim Kru licki Quits Pro Hockey."

I wasn't totally surprised because I'd grown to know Jim pretty well both when we were teammates earlier in the season and when I'd played against him as a Junior.

But here was a 23-year-old left winger who had finished the season with Detroit and who appeared to have a career ahead of him.

Consulting my diary, I read some notes I'd written about Krulicki when he was a Ranger. "He's a very deceptive skater. He's bouncy on his skates. Jim is gaining confidence and using some moves I've never seen before. He should come along fine."

Detroit figured to be a break for Jim because he'd get lots of ice time and develop into a solid hockey player. But as I read the story about him quitting, I realized that Jim had delivered a pretty strong indictment of professional hockey.

"My decision to quit pro hockey was not a hasty one," Jim said. "I've done much thinking about it for the past three years. There's nothing that can change my mind because the reasons are purely personal.

"There's no freedom playing professional hockey. Sure the money is good, but money isn't everything. I want to be happy and do the things I want when I'm still young.

"Simply, I'm not prepared to make the sacrifice required to excel at the game. Time is not your own. You can't relax. I don't want to be a machine which can be traded on the merits of people who sit around and discuss what I can do and what I can't do on a hockey rink.

"Very few people accept an athlete as a person or even try to—there's too much phoniness. They want to be around pro athletes so they can tell their friends, 'I know this guy and that guy and we did this and that.' It makes me sick to think about these bandwagon characters.

"Professional hockey is a ruthless business and the fun is gone out of the game. Hockey clubs want you to play even if you're hurt.

"Take that last season I played in Kitchener as a Junior. I was banged up with a bad knee and people thought I was faking. The next year, my first as a pro, proved them wrong. I underwent surgery and the doctor told me my knee was mangled so badly that a couple of more weeks and I wouldn't have to worry about playing hockey at all.

"Managers and coaches treat you like children. It's always do this, do that, don't be caught in such a place the night before a game. Don't patronize this bar or that bar.

"If all the players go together and have a few beers and somebody else wants to go off by himself and read a book, management thinks there's something wrong. You're not one of the boys."

Jim said he was going to continue his studies at the University of Waterloo, Ontario, and then go to Europe. "I'll probably miss pro hockey," he said, "but not to the extent I'll regret quitting."

Krulicki's words had great significance for me because we're both 23 years old, we both moved up through the Rangers' organization and we both made it to the NHL. But there the similarity ends. The basic difference between his quitting and my staying is that I have the determination and self-discipline, and Krulicki doesn't.

I don't have any illusions about the NHL. I know it's a big, ruthless business. My contract experience with Francis last summer convinced me of that. And unless a man reaches the top level, it's not worth playing hockey for money. Management doesn't give two hoots about anybody who expects to spend his career in the minors. They would rather get a veteran out and get a young guy in his spot whom they can develop.

Jim said he thought about quitting when he was a Junior. We all did. A Junior hockey player knows that if he wants to make a career out of the game he should plan to spend at least two years in the minors and then, if it appears he can't make the NHL, he should quit because life in the minors is just about the worst. You ride the bus, you get low pay and you're skating on a treadmill to oblivion.

Jim Krulicki had made it but he wasn't prepared to work. He wasn't dedicated, he never went overboard or really tried to excel.

Of course, some of Jim's beefs are sickeningly true. Management does overlook injuries at certain levels.

If a superstar hurts his knee, six doctors are called to attend him. If an unknown acquires a similar injury, he's told to "skate it out." And since hockey is a business, you must look after yourself.

Also, regimentation *is* a necessary part of hockey—just like the army. Unfortunately, it takes a certain amount of discipline to accomplish certain objectives.

Sure, discipline is onerous to a professional, but without discipline we all tend to go our separate ways. Unity is gone and we fall apart as a team. That's what happened to the Bruins last spring. Tom Johnson eased up and the Bruins were upset by the well-disciplined Canadiens.

At 23 Krulicki and I each made our choice. He selected the "mod" approach, and I don't blame him. Except I'm more traditional. I accept hockey's minuses as well as its pluses. The game is no honeymoon. It's fun, but it's also so incredibly grueling that I've been tempted to become a beachcomber.

But then I think of all the time and effort I've expended to fulfill my life's ambition—to play in the National Hockey League—and I realize there's merit to the words, "Sweet are the uses of adversity."

For Jim Krulicki, retirement from professional hockey is probably the best thing. But for Brad Park, who expects to be around another ten years or so at the very least, he'd like a spot of champagne from that Stanley Cup!